Praise for

Guide to Lasting Love

"Reta Faye Walker's *Guide to Lasting Love: A Therapist's 21-Day Program to a Fulfilling Relationship* is the perfect resource for anyone looking to reconnect or deepen their connection with their partner, build intimacy, and learn skills to create and maintain a healthy and fulfilling partnership. This book is thoughtful, trauma-informed, and offers practical tools to help you navigate your relationship with greater intention and care."

—Leah Aguirre, LCSW
Author of *Is This Really Love?* and
Featured Contributor for *GQ* and *Psychology Today*

"Walker delves deep into what it takes to make a bond not only last, but flourish. Chock-full of insight and inspiration, *Guide to Lasting Love* is a must-have tool for couples looking to revitalize their spark."

—Traci Morrow
Professional Marriage Mentor and Bestselling Author of
Real-Life Marriage: Navigating Your Beautiful, Messy, One-of-a-Kind Love Story

"*Guide to Lasting Love* is an exemplary guidebook for romantic relationships of any age. Walker writes with passion, fueled by the authentic, encompassing purpose of helping you cultivate the love and connection you deserve!"

—Jerry Giordano
Contentment Counselor, Former TEDx Producer, and Author of
Your 7 Words to a Happier You: Unlock the Story Sabotaging Your Relationships

"Reta Faye Walker has written a seminal relationship guide for couples. It goes without saying that this book has the potential of being an invaluable tool for any couple willing to commit to and benefit from a monumental guide to everlasting love."

—Dr. Dan Dalton, PhD, C. Psych.

Guide to Lasting Love

Guide to Lasting Love

A Therapist's 21-DAY Program to a FULFILLING RELATIONSHIP

Reta Faye Walker

BROWN BOOKS
PUBLISHING GROUP

© 2025 Reta Faye Walker

All rights reserved. No part of this book may be used or reproduced in any manner without written permission except in the case of brief quotations embodied in critical articles or reviews.

Note to the Reader: To protect the privacy and confidentiality of all counseling clients mentioned in this book, their names and any identifying details have been altered.

Guide to Lasting Love
A Therapist's 21-Day Program to a Fulfilling Relationship

Brown Books Publishing Group
Dallas, TX / New York, NY
www.BrownBooks.com
(972) 381-0009

A New Era in Publishing®

Publisher's Cataloging-In-Publication Data

Names: Walker, Reta Faye, author.
Title: Guide to lasting love : a therapist's 21-day program to a fulfilling relationship / Reta Faye Walker.
Description: Dallas, TX ; New York, NY : Brown Books Publishing Group, [2025] | Includes bibliographical references.
Identifiers: ISBN: 978-1-61254-697-1 (print) | 978-1-61254-698-8 (ebook) | LCCN: 2024947164
Subjects: LCSH: Marriage. | Interpersonal relations. | Couples therapy. | Love. | Intimacy (Psychology) | BISAC: FAMILY & RELATIONSHIPS / Love & Romance. | FAMILY & RELATIONSHIPS / Marriage & Long-Term Relationships. | SELF-HELP / Personal Growth / Happiness.
Classification: LCC: HQ734 .W35 2025 | DDC: 306.81--dc23

ISBN 978-1-61254-697-1
EISBN 978-1-61254-698-8
LCCN 2024947164

Printed in Canada
10 9 8 7 6 5 4 3 2 1

For more information or to contact the author, please go to www.RetaFayeWalker.com.

To the imperfect person in a difficult relationship.

To be fully seen by somebody, then, and to be loved anyhow—this is a human offering that can border on the miraculous.
—Elizabeth Gilbert

Table of Contents

Introduction. 1

Four Relationship Truths. 9

Day 1: Creating a Purpose-Driven Relationship 17

Day 2: Finding Hope. 29

Day 3: Growth Mindset 39

Day 4: Responding to Signals for Attention 53

Day 5: Making a Match of Different Personalities 65

Day 6: Ending Couple Wars. 79

Day 7: Intentional Communication Strategies. 95

Day 8: Moving from I to We 105

Day 9: Dealing with Criticism from Your Partner 117

Day 10: Addressing Your Own Critical Nature 129

Day 11: The Three Dos and Don'ts of Problem-Solving 137

Day 12: The Stubborn Problem 147

Day 13: Reducing Stress in Your Relationship 159

Day 14: The SHARE Principle 171

Day 15: The Unconscious Agenda 187

Day 16: A Deeper Look at Unmet Needs 199

Day 17: Working through Relationship Stages 209

Day 18: Five Strategies for Sex and Intimacy 217

Day 19: Intimacy Is More Than Sex 229

Day 20: Happiness Is Not Automatic 241

Day 21: Connection is the Key 249

Conclusion: Love Is Meant to Last 259

Acknowledgements 263

Notes 265

About the Author 275

Introduction: My Journey

I've always been fascinated by relationships. Seeing couples driving in a car, walking hand in hand, and sitting in a restaurant, I wanted to know why they were happy and how I could be as they were. I believed if I knew their stories, I could make a carbon copy and feel as they did. As a teenager, I drifted in and out of my friends' homes, spending more time with their parents than my friends, asking questions and viewing different lives and love stories. In time, I curated ideas of what I wanted, what I didn't want, and how I would get it.

In my drifting years, I observed two couples that defined good and bad coupling.

The first was an older couple, Maya and Con, the welcoming parents of my best friend at the time. Each evening they performed the same ritual of laughter and conversation in a shaded sunroom where they shared cocktails or tea and talked for hours. My memories are of her leaning in, his perpetual smile and eyes glued to hers. As children, we were privy to peals of laughter, giggles, gestures, and finally a move to the kitchen. Maya and Con were a bottomless well of joy and peace.

I also remember this couple facing tragedy and loss in their sunroom. This time the chairs were side by side, the conversation subdued, his arm drawing her even closer to catch all of their brokenness and sadness.

Another couple, young and in love, is locked in my memory, but for a different reason. Drew and Caroline were beautiful in a movie star kind of way, and as Caroline's wannabe little sister and friend, I had a front-row view into their lives. I frequented their usual haunts, romanticized their public displays of affection, and fantasized about them in a forever love story. However, a mere two years after the wedding, Drew rarely opened doors for Caroline, his eyes were flat and unaffected when she was around, and she seemed on the verge of tears almost anywhere. Within five years, they drifted into a polite truce destined to end badly.

These two couples epitomized for me the joy and sorrow of good and bad relationships. Their relationship behaviors defined what I did and didn't want.

But all of that was not enough to help me.

Openness and Trust

My first marriage ended in divorce for reasons other than disconnection or poor communication. I later realized that I hadn't let my significant other know me intimately. Not that I had hidden secrets, but I guarded my feelings, thoughts, and ideas, fearing they wouldn't be understood. We can consider the words of psychotherapist Beth Sonnenberg, who says that opening up regularly to our partners helps us get closer. "Once you think that your feelings don't matter, won't be heard, or are not worth sharing, you open the door to harbor negativity and resentment."[1] She is right, but I didn't know that then.

Undeterred, I jumped into marriage again, retaining the habits of self-protection without understanding the meaning and need for vulnerability, which would only come with my formal education in psychology, marriage, and family.

If openness and trust were my primary relationship lessons, they weren't obvious even to close family and friends to whom my husband and I seemed a golden couple. Is that familiar? Through the giddy wonder of the honeymoon years, these connection-busters weren't on my radar. But when the love chemicals settled down, I questioned things. I would think to myself, "He doesn't get me." Or, "Do I have to do it all?" Or, "What am I even doing here?"

At this point, it would have been easy to accept this as the reality of marriage or believe that I'd made a poor choice and find the exit doors. But I endured without embracing the necessary components of openness and trust, focusing instead on my career. I thrived in client relationships and began working with couples long before graduation day. By far the most memorable and formative instruction I had was my involvement with 112 divorcing couples. I was humbled by their stories of fighting, failures, crises, distress, and grief, and I became determined to help couples and families have happier relationships.

A common thread weaved itself between each story. Couples were unhappy and disconnected because they did not talk openly about their feelings, listened even less, and rarely experienced their spouse as safe and supportive. Without a high level of honesty and mutual acceptance, couples couldn't trust each other with their feelings and needs. They lived together as partners in child-rearing, bill paying, or friendship, but not as connected lovers.

This was an ideal opportunity for me to recognize my pattern of self-protection and disconnection. Here I was, helping others to communicate and connect, while living in a marriage that was happy only on the surface.

It wasn't until our children were leaving for university that I questioned the state of my relationship and wondered if I hadn't shortchanged my husband by being so "private" and so focused on work, home, and our children. When I started with the questions, my husband was surprised and confessed that it was easier to share feelings and be vulnerable with others than it was to me. He said, "You're the person people respect and admire but find it hard to warm up to."

My Epiphany

I pride myself on being authentic and a therapist who lives her calling as a conscious healer. So, as irritated as I was, I had to admit the truth in my husband's comment and accept that I had elevated stoicism to an art form.

Now I had to ask: What was I getting from swallowing my feelings and carrying my burdens alone? What was I avoiding by remaining a closed book? Answering these questions honestly meant revisiting the early-years experiences of being alone, disappointed but pretending that all was well. Then and now, I avoided the possibility of rejection, the shame of not being welcome, of being insignificant. Unconsciously, I was recreating these former experiences hoping for a different outcome—to find connection and experience real, warm, and loving feelings.

I now directed the full weight of my knowledge and experience as a therapist toward my own personal growth and change. To borrow a famously anonymous piece of wisdom, it was time for me "to be able at any moment to sacrifice what I am for what I could become." This journey began with writing a present-tense intention statement in my journal that challenged me to speak honestly and tactfully about feelings and thoughts. This new awareness and the desire to strengthen all my relationships prompted me to listen more closely and urge others to speak up. I began to prioritize engaging in conversation with my husband and our daughters with the goal of slowing down, awakening my curiosity, and speaking always with the goal of building my bond with the other. Change is never smooth, consistent, or always well received, but I was committed. Gradually I noticed that my responses to my husband and daughters became less angry and worried and more relaxed and productive, and I received a "thumbs-up" in many different ways.

Throughout my own relationship journeys, I have come to realize that we have all been led to believe that lasting love is automatic, and that we're greatly disappointed to discover it requires work. Many of us did not grow up in homes that modeled healthy bonding, conflict resolution, and respect for individual values or equity. The good news is that the work you put into your relationship will bring you to a surprising realization: experiencing conflict can be a gift that *invites* healthy and effective communication and can lead to strengthening the bond you share with your partner. The ever-strengthening connection that follows is the beginning of your *true* love story.

Doing This Course

The work of building a love that lasts can be challenging, as it requires looking deeply into our minds and hearts, courageously analyzing our upbringings and our previous relationship experiences, and shifting our beliefs about who we are and how love is supposed to be. Ultimately, the work of lasting love is a lifestyle that depends on daily devotion.

You can think of this guide as part relationship devotional and part educational tool. It combines research from my therapy practice with the wisdom of philosophers and positive psychology, as well as the work of leading experts, to solve the core issues that most often lead to the dissolution of intimate relationships. Designed as a step-by-step process bolstered with concrete communication strategies and action plans, it can help even the busiest and most distant couples stop relationship breakdown in its tracks.

There is no wrong or right way to approach the course. If you do it as a daily exercise, try to reserve thirty minutes or longer to allow for discussion and reflection together. You may even choose to do it weekly or on a different schedule altogether, depending on your needs and availability. I do recommend that you commit to the 21-day process by going through each day in numbered sequence, and returning later to review the chapters that speak to the specific issues you currently face. This guide promotes an interactive process of relationship building, so it's suggested that you use a notebook to journal your questions, new insights, and results of activities.

Before beginning, consider the following guidance to help aid your journey through this program.

Pace the Work to Your Needs and Abilities

When working with your partner, it is acceptable to table any disagreement that you can't seem to make any headway on; instead, write down the details of your disagreement in your respective journals, and agree to collaborate again on this disagreement at a later time. This applies especially if your partner becomes upset by the reminder of a painful event. In either case, reserve some time to journal about the distress as soon as possible. Ask yourself the following questions and write your answers:

- Why did we have to pause our conversation?
- Why am I feeling sad, angry, or hurt?
- What can I do right now to calm myself?

The further along in your journey through this guide, the better equipped you will be to answer such questions with greater insight and a more effective vocabulary to speak about your feelings and experiences. In the meantime, each of you should continue to journal your thoughts and questions regarding your disagreement to have handy when you're both ready to return to the conversation.

Meanwhile, make an effort to remind yourselves that major differences, even between intimate partners, is normal. Try to perceive your disagreements not as roadblocks, but as opportunities for reflection, for asking helpful questions, and for fostering mutually rewarding discussions.

Of course, we're all living our lives, and it may be challenging for us at times to stay focused throughout the program. You may be distracted with your weekly obligations, or a sudden crisis; you may even question whether you are truly committed to building a lasting love with your partner. At any of these junctures, I only ask that you do some soul-searching and make every effort not to abandon love. If a particular section in this guide doesn't seem to apply to you at the moment, move past it with a note to return to it later. If another seems too intense to engage with or too difficult to apply at the moment, you can also return, allowing yourself more time to engage later. In the case of a true life crisis, it is of course suggested that you deal with that situation and return to the agenda when you are ready.

And at any time, please seek the support of a therapist or friend if the process becomes too difficult for you and your partner.

Anticipate Resistance

When we are immersed in any process of change and growth, we often feel the tug of ambivalence and hesitation as we shift out of our comfort zones. It is then that we must "talk back" to our voice of fear and discomfort and seek the courage to stay motivated and keep a clear vision of our goals.

Embrace Imperfection

Nothing is accomplished when we require perfection of ourselves or others. That glass ceiling is never attainable, and it dissolves before our eyes when we focus on the tasks of empathy and self-compassion.

Dear reader, you who want more than anything to pass your days with the one who warms your heart, to be called "Beloved," and to discover lasting peace in your bond—take heart. *You are not alone.* You may be here as a beginner, hungry to do it right. Or you may be checking in for timely reminders, tool sharpening, or a long-needed pep talk.

Right now, your relationship may be testing the very limits of your strength. You may be feeling fragile beyond belief, unsure even of what step to take next. We may feel the desperation of philosopher Thomas Merton, who pleaded, "My Lord God, I have no idea where I am going. I do not see the road ahead of me. I cannot know for certain where it will end." But the fact that you are here and trying is all you need to assure you—you've already begun the process of healing and rebuilding. Welcome! You are part of a community of imperfect people; whatever your struggles, remember that you are seen and loved.

In twenty-plus years of practice, I have used the following guidance to help hundreds of couples not only step back onto the paths of their relationships, but be able to see that the road that lies ahead of them can be one of fulfilling, lasting love. You can too.

Four Relationship Truths

Before we begin the 21-day program, we must first understand the four "magical truths" of relationships. The four magical truths are the pillars from which all of this book's guidance flows. We call them "magical" not because they're fantastical, but because when we embrace them and integrate them into our relationship behaviors, they seem to magically produce the right conditions for building a lasting love with our partners. In fact, the magical truths remind us that not only are we human, but that we must exist *as* humans within our relationships and not as impossible ideals of what humans should be.

The four magical truths are not universally accepted; perhaps that's because while elegantly simple in concept, it takes hard work and ongoing dedication to adhere to them. Each magical truth challenges us to take on specific relationship skills. Just remember that, as with all newly learned skills, the more you practice, the easier they come.

Magical Truth #1:
Your Partner Is Doing the Best They Can

Paul and Jana have been together for twelve years, and Paul is still frustrated that Jana is late for everything. The fight they have is like a movie on repeat. He starts worrying a few hours before an event and asks her if she can be on time. She promises that she will. But then Jana finds something important to do at the last minute. A fight ensues. This happens over and over, and occasionally the fight erupts into name-calling and character-slamming. Everything changed one year when Paul was host at his office Christmas party. A few hours before the party he explained to Jana that he would leave at 6:00 p.m. and she could arrive at her convenience. This became the new accepted practice for the couple. Paul released all expectations of Jana. The boundary he set allowed him to be compassionate, generous, and helpful, and opened the door for more fruitful conversations with Jana about why it was important to him that she be on time for events.

We can all think of someone who we believe is not doing the best they can and our reaction to that person is anger, frustration, and even resentment. Imagine feeling that way about your significant other. Is that a feeling you hide by drawing the curtains behind your eyes, clenching your teeth, or walking away? Or worse, you respond to their faults with criticism and contempt. When we are faced with daily frustrations, occasional mishaps, behavior, or values different from our own, we have the choice to be negative or positive. Being positive means adopting a fresh mindset that is generous and compassionate, and reminding yourself that your partner is doing the best they can.

Most of us want the other person to change, get it right, and work with us. Our ego screams, "I am right, do things my way, make me happy." Social psychologist Elliot Aronson says this motivational force of "self-justification," or the ego, plays a central role in our lives.[1] This means that when our significant other sees the world through a different lens, our instinct is to say they are wrong, placing ourselves in the stance of nonacceptance. But we have the other option of calming the ego and allowing the other person autonomy in their own behavior.

What is especially helpful to the partner who embraces this truth is that the kindness and nonjudgment they extend will reach back to their own self. So, they can finally release their own unreasonable and perfectionist demands of themselves and enjoy being "good enough."

I am not suggesting that we accept our significant other's bad habits and suppress our anger and hurt to create further stress and trauma in our lives. Avoiding the truth, making excuses for, and accepting bad behavior is harmful to you and your relationship. We need to have the courage to speak up against distressing, hurtful activities, especially emotional or physical abuse. If we don't, we exist in codependence and blind compassion, which Robert Augustus Masters, reformed cult leader and author of *Spiritual Bypassing*, describes well:

> With blind compassion we don't know how to—or won't learn how to—say "no" with any real power, avoiding confrontation at all costs and, as a result, enabling unhealthy patterns to continue. Our "yes" is then anemic and impotent, devoid of the impact it could have if we were also able to access a clear, strong "no" that emanated from our core. When we mute our essential voice, our openness is reduced to a permissive gap, an undiscerning embrace, a poorly boundaried receptivity, all of which indicate a lack of compassion for ourselves . . . [2]

Speaking up, expressing anger and hurt, and setting boundaries allow you to stay relationship-healthy while accepting that your significant other is doing the best they can. When we do this with kindness, we honor ourselves and our significant other.

Magical Truth #2:
Your Mindset Can Make or Break a Relationship

As hard as it is to imagine, a shift in mindset can be all it takes to start a new journey or change direction, and it is imperative in a relationship in trouble or one that needs a tweak. Two things are important in a relationship-building mindset: a growth mindset and a positive outlook.

Growth Mindset

Since the launch in 2006 of Carol Dweck's famous book, *Mindset: The New Psychology of Success,* individuals, progressive leaders, and successful couples have embraced the idea that their failures were learning opportunities and their efforts were a significant factor in progress. For the couple with a "growth mindset," a term used by Dweck, success is working to be your best and not about establishing superiority or worth. Imagine the painful experience of being in a relationship with someone who is condescending, patronizing, and even pompous!

Dweck says the fixed mindset promotes harmful myths in a relationship. Chief among these is the myth of "happily ever after," and that a relationship shouldn't take work because each partner should simply know how the other feels.[3] The difficulty doesn't stop there; it moves into either self- or partner-blame for character flaws and inevitably to anger, disgust, and contempt. Finally, since the problem is inherent and fixed, it can't be solved. Dweck summarizes her findings about relationships by saying,

> when people embark on a relationship, they encounter a partner who is different from them, and they haven't learned how to deal with the differences. In a good relationship, people develop these skills and, as they do, both partners grow, and the relationship deepens. But for this to happen, people need to feel they're on the same side . . . As an atmosphere of trust developed, they [become] vitally interested in each other's development.[4]

Positivity

The brain is biased negatively. This is a protective instinct. Very few people look on the bright side. What that means is in relationships, after the first blush of romance, you tend to notice your partner's faults, real or imagined, and ignore your own. We remember their criticism more than we recall our significant other's compliments. When Roy Baumeister, an American social psychologist, asked his students why they thought they would be a good partner, they listed positive things but neglected the crucial element in a couple's alliance—avoiding the negative. He says that "being able to hold your tongue rather than say something nasty or spiteful will do much more for your relationship than a good word or deed."[5] So the next time your loved one doesn't put away the laundry or when you don't exactly share their opinion or values, let it go for the moment and consider more effective means to achieving your goals.

Loving another through good and bad, in sickness and in health, is no small ask and only possible in a climate free from negativity. Criticism, contempt, name-calling, and unkindness are only a few ways that relationships drift into apathy and despair.

Magical Truth #3:
Your Relationship Depends on a Paradox

The more we can depend on and trust our partners, the more independent we can be.

This is just one of the many paradoxes couples face in their relationships. North American culture has demonized dependency and left us believing that a healthy person is an independent, self-sufficient one who can find happiness and self-fulfillment from within. Any signs of need are therefore perceived as a deficiency. However, attachment theory and recent research teaches us that it is natural and healthy to have a reciprocal dependency or interdependency. Individuals and relationships thrive when a couple relies on one another. To further complicate our thinking is the term *codependency*, which is also lumped negatively with dependency, and couples who buy into the belief that they must function independently are in danger of disconnection.

The inconsistencies that a paradox in your relationship produces are not a problem except when they lead to confusion about how to navigate life with your significant other. Other examples of paradoxes include:

If I take responsibility for my actions, I will be trusted/forgiven. If I release my need for trust/forgiveness, knowing that responsibility is the right action, I may have to accept the outcome, whatever it is.

The more I give, the more others demand. I can continue to be generous and say no when necessary.

The more I focus on my desires, needs, and ideals the less they seem to get met. I am responsible for attaining my desires, needs, and ideals and don't expect others to have the same commitment to them.

The partner that is less invested gets more attention. I can manage where I focus my energy and attention.

If I am calm and kind, they will cooperate. My decision to be calm and kind is more likely to gain the cooperation of others but doesn't guarantee it.

The key to navigating through paradox is to somewhat, if not completely, release absolute truths and appreciate those truths relative to the person, the needs of the situation, or the requirement of a loving heart. This does not mean that the absolute truth does not exist but that it must coexist with the relative truth.

Sometimes we don't like the paradoxes we face, or they don't seem fair. They may even contradict the significant lessons of your life so far. Discerning and reframing the distinct paradox in your relationship will release you from unnecessary relationship angst, prevent unhelpful and negative labeling, and allow you to have a wide-angle-lens view of your life together.

Magical Truth # 4:
Words Without Purposeful and Wholehearted Action Are Ineffective

We begin our relationships with words, but if they never become grounded in action, we are left with broken promises and broken trust. Our actions toward our significant other, therefore, must include self-management and fulfill the needs of the relationship. Without this behavior in place, one partner carries the weight of the relationship and says, "I can't do this anymore."

Healthy self-management is present when a partner hears and responds to the word "no" without complaints or attempts to control or manipulate. Even when coercion is gentle or humorous, it still sends a message that the other person's needs and wants are unimportant or less valuable than yours. Poor self-management can range into abusive behavior, even addiction, and can violate the core value of safety and security that every relationship must have.

There are other ways in which a lack of action can break down a relationship. Consider a relationship where a partner's focus is primarily on themselves. They don't listen attentively to learn about the other, to remember their favorite color, or to share hopes for the future and treasured dreams. They forget or ignore special, and even normal, occasions, rarely surprise the other with a gift, or make the other a priority in their plans. They walk away when they most need a shoulder to cry on or a listening ear. They don't initiate help or get things done without being asked. What's worse, they break promises and border on dishonesty.

Even the most thoughtful or well-written words unaccompanied by actions are empty.

Every relationship, even strong ones, might reveal this type of inaction at some point. But it's by taking action in these ways that you build a strong relationship.

> *Love is a verb. Without action, it is merely a word.*
> —Unknown

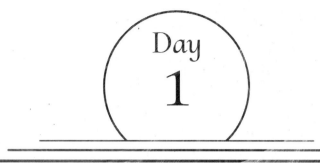

Creating a Purpose-Driven Relationship

Is this familiar?

You've realized that you've been more and more regularly asking yourself, "Why am I in this relationship? What am I getting from this relationship? Am I fulfilling my life's purpose?"

I work with many couples who are asking these very questions. In Day 1, we'll go over such questions in depth and, through answering them, discover how you can create a purpose-driven relationship.

On a late September night many years ago, I pondered the reason for being in my marriage, for all my effort and patience, even down to making meals and housekeeping, wondering if it was worthwhile. I questioned *the point of it all*—just as I have heard others do many times since. I wasn't old enough, but here I was in a midlife crisis, pondering the state of my marriage.

Raising kids and pursuing a career meant time for reflection was rare, but the questions persisted as I dashed frantically from one task to another. Somehow, sandwiched between the rush to get dinner on the table and chauffeur my children around, I devoted time to seek knowledge to help me understand my feelings. Books about goal setting, achievement, positive thinking, and relationships spilled from the nightstand beside my bed. I completed personality tests and questionnaires to help me clarify values, needs, and wants. I attended seminars offering personal growth and the motivation to be all I could be. Finally, exhausted and dissatisfied, I released my angst to the wastebasket of unfinished self-development. I hoped that someday I would know what I was doing in this marriage and why it was significant.

A few years later, against a complicated backdrop of caregiving and hardship, raunchy family humor, pie baking, and trying hard not to cheat at Monopoly, I resumed the effort to find purpose in my marriage. Reading autobiographies and books on philosophy and spirituality and pursuing a meditation practice helped broaden my perspective. Finally, the answers evolved in a way that felt more honest, truthful, and noble than they had in the past. They brought "lift" to me and our marriage.

I learned that as human beings we have a calling—a reason for being that is more significant than pleasing parents, landing the right job, or getting rich. This calling demands making contributions and taking responsibility, and nowhere is it more needed than in a relationship. Through this realization I was able to answer my three questions and inspire couples to have conversations about mission and purpose.

Why Am I in This Relationship?

I've learned that I bring unique qualities to my marriage—qualities I've unknowingly cultivated and honed for relationships into my adulthood. They include being optimistic, detail-oriented, and balanced, and they complement my husband's drive and ambition. As I focus on our mutual contribution to ourselves, our children, and our families, I feel "on purpose." Having a "why" helped me chart a life course and decide on the how, what, when, and where.

My clients Angie and Emile also needed to discover a worthy "why" when their relationship fell apart. They came to me at a crisis point, with Emile saying, "I wouldn't stay married if we didn't have children."

Both came from traditional homes and upwardly mobile families, so they embraced the pressures to succeed financially and socially and were on track to a traditional life: a nuclear family, good careers, and happily ever after.

Their disconnection, fighting, and growing disappointment began in the early stages of wedding planning, but the couple forged ahead, believing if they checked the right boxes all would be well. After having two children and lives packed with activities, Emile settled into his life at work and flirted with his female colleagues while Angie immersed herself in Facebook groups and the lonely work of parenting alone. They seemed outwardly happy, but their relationship was a struggle. Emile's comment was, "Every conversation ends in a fight. I don't know why we are together."

The couple's relationship improved when they learned to communicate better and had regular date nights, but it wasn't until their conversations explored the question of their purpose and mission together that they created a secure foundation.

Many couples might see themselves in the story of Angie and Emile. Their natural instinct was establishing themselves financially, cultivating friendships and acceptance with their peers, relaxing with movies and games, and seeking novel experiences. While these activities are acceptable, a couple will need more when they interface with success and failure, crossing paths with birth, death, betrayal, promise, and hope. Each partner will need to know "why" they work the long hours, why they concede an argument, why both might feel they support someone else's dream. Ultimately, the couple will need a foundation for experiencing true "membership" in their relationship, where each partner gets an equal vote and the family needs override their own.

What Am I Getting from the Relationship?

I have learned that in a relationship I must give and get equally, and that I can make a real difference. It is also important within a marriage that each partner has a safe place for personal growth, the latitude to make mistakes, learn from them, and live as a community.

We can learn the value of this "marriage community," where both partners give and get equally, from Brent's story.

At forty-five, Brent was a successful financial planner who was described as "having it all." He recently bought a sports car to join the twin SUV parked next to his wife's. The couple lived in an expensive home, she enjoyed a solid career, and their children were healthy, active, and thriving. But away from the scrutiny of others, Brent was desperately unhappy, always seeking the next win, and at times engaging in risky behavior. He soon recognized that he had scripted his life with his parents' values as they "guided" him into success.

Brent began to neglect his family and his work and seemed determined to veer away from what he had built in an attempt to "live his best life." I don't doubt that many like Brent want to leave the constraints of a scripted life and start fresh. Many are in danger of throwing the baby out with the bathwater, so to speak—throwing away a marriage and family because it seems like a trap where they feel overworked and unfulfilled. With that in mind, I asked Brent to do some soul-searching before leaving his job, wife, and family. Borrowing from the basic concepts of logotherapy, I reminded him: ·

1. We have freedom of choice on how to respond to life, but we are personally responsible for those actions.
2. The desire to find meaning is worthwhile and could prevent a decline in mental health.
3. We are fulfilled when we contribute and give, not when we grasp and take what we "think we deserve."

In his journaling Brent ended up asking big life questions: When did I start wanting to escape? What am I running away from? What am I running to?

Can I make changes and be responsible to the people who depend on me?

What will I be leaving behind?

In answering those last questions, Brent had an aha moment: he had lost focus on what he was getting from a relationship with his wife, her value in his life.

What I observed in Brent, as I do in many of us approaching middle adulthood, is how easy it is to lose motivation and energy when we have acquired a home, cars, and the trappings of success. It's as if we flounder without those pressing goals and an immediate and clear trajectory upward. We are confused when there is no familiar carrot to entice. As a result, we can bias negatively and blame the relationship we feel we don't need to "work" for. When the flow of romance pales, we cast around for something, or someone, to captivate our attention.

Purpose and meaning are fundamental human needs; when we have achieved our basic needs, our pilgrimage into this deeper fulfillment begins. Neglecting our drive for purpose and meaning means we risk cycling through "getting things" to feel good or stumbling in confusion without knowing the source of our unhappiness.

I kept tabs on Brent's journey in our regular meetings and was encouraged to note that he had taken responsibility for his own life through depression management and had involved his wife in preparing for a career change. He was participating in family activities again and ensuring that the changes he made would be manageable. In his continual journey to meaning and purpose, Brent has continued to invite Marianne, his wife, to envision with him their best possible life and to set intersecting goals.

Am I Fulfilling My Purpose?

I discovered a sense of purpose as I served, loved, shaped, and was served, loved, shaped in return. Making mistakes, trying again, feeling remorse, gaining insight, and being responsible are solid steps for the kind, thoughtful, grounded, and wise human being to fulfill a larger purpose.

A committed romantic relationship is the most crucial endeavour in your adult life, and no other arena challenges your personality and character as this does. Without expecting to, you expand, prune, and mold each other as you become well-rounded and practice a full range of human qualities. In a secure relationship, I could explore my creative interests, expand my skills, and grow into a purpose-filled person.

Mary is an example of someone who was suffering personally by not addressing the stressors in her marriage and was too afraid to admit that something was wrong. She was currently unemployed and wasting her significant talent leading a mediocre life. She alternated between depression and confusion with a crutch statement: "I just don't know what's wrong!"

For Mary, I adapted "life-crafting" to help her find meaning in her life and in her relationship. The originators of the concept describe life-crafting as "a process of reflecting on one's values, passions and goals, best possible self, and goal attainment plans."[1]

I distilled this into three questions for Mary to clarify and answer:

1. What values, passions, and goals can I meet in my relationship? ·
2. How can I live my best possible self in it?
3. What do I need in the future to maintain a fulfilled life and relationship?

Mary ultimately returned to a personal life filled with purpose and satisfaction. Her real success, however, was in her ability to include her husband in her progress and together reimagine their life in a way that guaranteed the success of the home. This happened through conversations guided by their morals, values, ethics, and beliefs as well as their hopes and dreams.

Excerpt

The part of you seeking purpose in a relationship doesn't say, "I am here to get as much support and care as I can."

It speaks, rather, in the plural and sounds more like, "We are here to give and take love, care, and support."

Through my own reflections and the stories of couples I helped, you can begin to see how to find purpose in your relationship. Your reflections may be different, but in finding your answers you find purpose, which in turn builds your relationship.

The "Why" behind Finding Purpose

After the honeymoon, when couples begin to navigate reality, power struggles, disappointments, and the challenges of a long-term relationship, they need to ask and answer questions that justify their life together, bring significance and value to their efforts, and offer a compelling compass point on their path. Without this focus on purpose, Angie, Brett, and Mary risk drifting along into a reactive frame of mind and responding to hardships and hurt with bitterness and resentment.

The *raison d'être* of relationship purpose is to shift away from boredom, dissatisfaction, and relationship drift. With your own created focus, you are more likely to solve resentments and arguments.

Purpose from Cradle to Grave

When a five-year-old is doing what he loves to do, he is living his purpose. Erik Erikson, one of the most influential child psychoanalysts of the twentieth century, says that if a child learns to trust and has the freedom to do so, he shows initiative and ambition during the preschool years, demonstrating purpose.[2] Evident in your earliest years, your sense of life's purpose is refined over time and will only change if others try to push and correct it so that you feel ashamed of your choices and try too hard to please.

As a teen, the venue for purpose expands beyond the home to school or a team. You may bring laughter, focus, order, diligence, or all of the above to your peers. Others may even benefit from the clarity of your purpose.

In adulthood, the desire to be in a romantic relationship intensifies, and how you bond, give, and seek love will be crucial to relationship success. You can choose to neglect your relationship and consistently make your needs a priority to win at any cost. You can create chaos, leaving someone broken, wounded, and damaged. All the while, you'll be ignoring what should be the impetus that fuels lasting love.

Without a clear identification of purpose, you risk falling into the habit of manipulation, getting your way by abusing words like *sacrifice* and *compromise*, taking as much as you can, and giving as little as possible. Ignoring your life's purpose may also lead to mental health issues, addiction, and a pattern of poor choices in general.

If that is the case, stop now, reflect, and discover the purpose already within you. You are born with a purpose and everything you need to fulfill that purpose.

To paraphrase Viktor Frankl, psychiatrist and founder of logotherapy, life's meaning lies in finding a purpose and taking responsibility for ourselves and other human beings.[3]

Excerpt

With a clear "why" we can face all of the "how" questions of life. Only by feeling free and sure of the objective that motivates us will we make the world a better place.

Putting It into Practice

I've found there are five strategies to help find greater purpose in your relationship and improve communication and intimacy.

Participation

Remembering Emile and Angie, the more engaged they were, the more meaningful their project of purpose was to their children and themselves. When they were distracted and detached they lost momentum. Each person's contributions fluctuated at times, one person sometimes offering more than the other; and sometimes their contributions were just different. The vacations that Angie planned might include a museum, while Emile delivered fun, adventure, and a passion for sports. Their personality, life experiences, and individual talents made the purpose in the relationship unique and gave each person influence that might not have surfaced otherwise.

Respect

Remembering Brent and Marianne, they realized that they not only ignored but were also negative and condescending to each other. So a good starting point in their search for relationship purpose was to think of and treat each other as unique and irreplaceable. This meant changing their interactions, thoughts, and attitudes. What followed was a progression to contributing more and owning up when each were at fault.

A Question: Personal Responsibility

Ask yourself how your relationship could change if it were all up to you. Taking personal responsibility and making real contributions are at the heart of a life full of meaning.

A Reminder: Life Balance

Busyness, stress, and distraction throw our lives out of balance and are the silent enemies of relationships.

Other Focus

In a world where we tend to find meaning in presenting a "perfect life" through posts, selfies, excess posturing, achievements, and activity in general, the idea of thoughtfully seeking purpose and meaning may seem a bit lame. Even the prevalence of YOLO and FOMO ("You Only Live Once" and "Fear of Missing Out") is at odds with the idea of looking within. But my experiences with couples prove that being half-in and half-out of a good relationship will not inspire lasting love.

Consider the following statements about purpose in a relationship and reflect on how they may be true in your case:

- A sense of purpose doesn't make the relationship easy. A lifetime with your significant other can be demanding and require sacrifice.

- Living with purpose is something you do, even when there is no extrinsic reward.
- Despite difficulties, purpose brings joy and confidence. You feel "in the zone."
- Living from a sense of purpose allows you to live without pretense and discover your vulnerability.
- Living "on purpose" makes a difference in the lives of the people around you.

One of my favorite examples of living with purpose in a relationship comes from a sixty-seven-year-old man who entered my office in May 2019, grieving his wife's death after forty-two years together. Through tears, he asked me to read a letter she had written to him a few days before she died.

Dear Harold,

I have no complaints about life. You were the kindest man, and I knew I could depend on you no matter what. You provided for us and allowed me the freedom to do the things that made me happy. Thank you for the many great years together.

With love,
Jennie

When we isolate ourselves from relationships, our ability to live on purpose is blunted. It is through our partners, however, that we can make the world a better place. In turn, we benefit from a world that contributes to our lives. Ultimately, everyone works within a relationship of one kind or another to fulfill their purpose.

Reflection | Day 1:
Creating A Purpose-Driven Relationship

Points to Remember
Your contribution to your partner's life molds your character and personality. While sharing your gifts, you are shaping and being shaped.

Questions to Ask
- What is your purpose in your relationship?
- What distracts you from your purpose?
- Are you fulfilling your purpose?

Action Plan
Write the letter you want your partner to give you after twenty-five years together. List the changes that will ensure this letter is authentic. Share the letter with your significant other and express the changes you wish to make to help you fulfill your relationship purpose.

Finding Hope

Is this familiar?

You feel helpless to repair the mistakes of the past with your partner. Every attempt to address an issue seems to be met with a roadblock.

I meet many couples who say, "We have made so many mistakes. Can we rebuild where there was no foundation?" It may not be easy, but it is possible. Day 2 takes you through the steps to find hope.

Hurt often occurs in a relationship through ignorance—either because a couple's life in the post-honeymoon period has no script, or because it has no frame of reference. Such a couple may have no example to follow at their disposal, no instructions to take from a trusted source, or have given no real thought of their responsibility to one another. So, after repeated infractions and disappointments they find themselves saying, "We have made so many mistakes. Can we rebuild when there was no foundation?" The answer is yes, they can learn to be a happy couple.

With a genuine desire to repair their bond, couples can navigate through challenges and emerge stronger than before. But each partner will need the courage and wisdom to be consistent when the other's behavior is illogical or emotional, and each will need the determination to stay the course as long as the couple wants to heal together.

Steps to Repairing Your Bond

Repairing a breach in your relationship requires thoughtful responses followed by deliberate action. These thoughtful responses are:
- Acknowledging the damage caused
- Taking responsibility
- Understanding the root of the issue
- Listening actively
- Expressing empathy

Acknowledge the Damage Caused

Initiating a reset usually begins with your partner's complaints, and though you may have yours as well, set them aside to make the necessary thoughtful responses and deliberate actions. Take Gail and Harry, for example. They are in a second marriage with adult children from previous relationship. Harry has felt Gail's withdrawal over the years, a withdrawal due to his speaking about her children's failures and treating them with contempt. Harry taking the responsibility to say, "I can see how I have hurt you by pointing out your son's mistakes," was a good beginning for this couple. Regardless of the issue, we must not excuse our harmful actions but acknowledge our part in causing hurt in our partner.

Take Responsibility

An acknowledgement of the damage he caused was a good first step for Harry, but following up with, "I was wrong to judge a young man so harshly and without compassion," told Gail this was more than the usual Band-Aid apology she had become used to.

Understand the Root of the Issue

With a commitment to personal growth, Harry initiated counseling to address his critical nature and inclination toward black-and-white thinking. Such thinking resulted in his judging "the world" harshly—Harry's world being Gail and her sons, the latter being especially easy targets.

Practice Active Listening

In the days following, Harry encouraged Gail to talk about the feelings that led to her withdrawal, and she eventually described her unwillingness to expose herself to his harsh criticism. It was Harry's active-listening approach that allowed her to feel safe to share honestly.

Express Empathy

Putting himself in her shoes and setting aside his own ideals of child-rearing allowed Harry the ability to say, "Knowing you as I do, I can see how my criticism would cause you to withdraw."

With the right attitude and genuine expressions of remorse, Harry and Gail were on the road to reconnection. The following thoughtful responses paved the way for the follow-through of acting deliberately.

"I can see how I have hurt you by pointing out your son's mistakes."

"I was wrong to judge a young man so harshly and without compassion."

"Knowing you as I do, I can see how my criticism would cause you to withdraw."

As invaluable as these responses are, however, they must be followed by deliberate actions that include apologizing, making amends, practicing forgiveness, recommitting fully, and rebuilding together.

Apologizing Sincerely

After a mistake, saying, "I am sorry," is the right next step, but you may find it challenging. It is the quality of your apology, though, that will make or break your effort to get your relationship back on track. Let's unpack the apology-reset connection and see why saying these three words is essential.

An earnest apology validates and justifies the person wronged, restoring their value. It opens the door to mutual compassion and empathy.

Saying you are sorry restores trust and belief that a relationship with you is viable and safe. Since your partner's sense of safety is a confirmation of your availability, your responsiveness, your true concern for them, and your promise to stay close (what we will later refer to as the "ARMS" of connection), your bond grows stronger.

A genuine apology resolves one person's hurt and the other's guilt. It opens the door to forgiveness and ends resentment.

Without an apology, there is no effective resolution or foundation laid for problem-solving.

Apologizing Thoughtfully

In a culture of over-apologizing, partners might take excessive responsibility. It is kind to be sorry for someone's hardship but unnecessary to take responsibility for what you haven't caused. An apology for what you are not responsible for sends a message of deference and passivity.

Don't apologize to end an argument or avoid a healthy confrontation. The danger is that this makes you the "fall guy" when your significant other is out of sorts, creating an unfair bias against you. Another risk is that you miss an opportunity to negotiate, solve problems, and draw closer. Conflict is unavoidable and even necessary between two people.

Another instance where a quick apology is a hindrance is when you use it merely to soothe and silence your significant other. If you are uncomfortable with your partner's justified emotions, admit your uneasiness and talk about that instead of apologizing as a ploy to "change the subject."

Don't apologize for your preferences, choices, and interests because they are different from theirs. You have a right to your quirks and to be fully yourself. Neither should you apologize for something unavoidable, unless you hurt someone. For example, standing too close to someone in a crowded room, making a commonly minor mistake, or choosing an unfamiliar pronunciation in mixed conversation does not require an apology.

Apologizing Emphatically and Empathically

In many years of face-to-face counseling, I have witnessed apologies made defensively, grudgingly, casually, carelessly, or so qualified as to be meaningless. Unless we are "all in" and prepared to set aside our selfish interests and engage emphatically and empathically with the other, we should not initiate an apology. To do otherwise leaves your partner feeling betrayed and insignificant.

A stand-alone "I am sorry" may be all you need to say for a minor infraction. But when you have done severe harm, you need to do more. At that point you must expand upon "I am sorry" in a way that acknowledges the extent of the damage you've done and how much you've hurt the other person:

"I am sorry that I lied about staying late at work. I can understand why you felt betrayed when you found out I had drinks with friends. Lying was a poor choice that I won't make again."

Don't make excuses.

Take the initiative and own up as soon as possible after an offense, while respecting the other person's need to process your apology before responding to you. If some time has already passed, don't hesitate any longer to elaborate. Keep eye contact and be sincere with your words, body language, and facial expressions—these gestures all must mirror the content of your heartfelt apology.

Remove your ego from the apology and avoid making excuses that will do your apology irreparable harm.

Examine these oft-used statements that make an apology ineffectual:

- Why do I have to say I am sorry?
- You are wrong too.
- I am not *entirely* wrong.
- You should apologize first.
- It's not a big deal.
- I have had to get over worse things.
- You won't forgive me anyway.

Can you say "I am sorry" without the urge to manipulate the other person or manage the results of your apology? When is saying "I am sorry" an abuse of the other person's good nature? Both the giver and the receiver of the apology must consider whether it was a tactic to stall a resolution or an expression of genuine remorse and a catalyst for change.

Making Amends

You know your significant other is genuine when they take action and make a consistent effort to change their mindset and thus their behavior. These actions are the engine behind restoring balance and trust in any relationship.

Equally necessary to the process of starting over is forgiveness.

Forgiving

We say we forgive, but I have met many who are bound to their exes by cords of unforgiveness long past the time when grieving should have brought fresh insight, wisdom, and a new direction. Patricia was such a person. Facing her fiftieth birthday, far too many conversations trailed into the infidelity, insensitivity, and the heartbreak she suffered twenty-five years ago. Her hurt and tears were still close to the surface, as was the question, "How *could* he?"—a question asked and answered many years before. Patricia tried dating but didn't trust anyone and left most relationships before the other person could disappoint her. Patricia traced her depression, anxiety, weight gain, and chronic fatigue to her husband's exit.

John Hopkins psychiatrist Karen Swartz says that forgiveness is necessary for good health.[1] She says that people who are stuck in or easily triggered into states of unforgiveness will experience harmful, chronic adrenaline highs that lead to high blood pressure, anxiety, depression, and a depressed immune system. Swartz makes it clear that forgiveness doesn't mean reconciliation to someone who can't be trusted or is unsafe, nor does it mean blind forgetting. She points out, though, that just challenging yourself to form a feeling of empathy and compassion for the person who has wronged you can be beneficial to your health.

> *Forgiveness doesn't excuse their behavior. Forgiveness prevents their behavior from destroying your heart.*
> —Unknown

Forgiveness is choosing your significant other's goodness over their faults in an effort to reconnect—you only need to flex the forgiveness muscle. Very few of us look forward to a workout at the gym but we all want the tone and power that comes with flexing and training our muscles. The act of forgiveness requires us to "flex" and activate the healthy parts of our minds. We flex when we see others as worthy of empathy and compassion; we flex to appreciate that we ourselves have at times needed forgiveness; we flex to think about the forgiven person positively and speak of them well—and we flex to give us the strength to say, "I forgive," as often as needed into the future. Forgiveness is the ultimate gift of grace.

The most poignant and public act of forgiveness was felt by the whole world when Nelson Mandela was released from prison and determined not to seek revenge but to forgive and work with his enemies to build a unified South Africa. What did he lose and what did he have to forgive? Nelson Mandela spent twenty-seven years in prison because he protested apartheid, entering a young man and exiting a much older one—years he would never get back, years spent in isolation, deprived of friends and family and even basic human rights.

Yet Mandela is remembered as saying, "Forgiveness liberates the soul. It removes fear. That is why it is such a powerful weapon."[2]

The Path to Forgiveness

Forgiveness is not a forgetting or a denial but a conscious, thoughtful decision that only an injured person can make. It should be unforced and is best accompanied by a mindful release of negative feelings. Follow these steps to practice forgiveness, remembering all along that you have 100 percent autonomy in the decision to forgive:

Remember: Bring to mind the incident or incidents you intend to forgive. It may help to write a letter to the person expressing your hurt, anger, and any other emotions that you feel or have felt in the past. You can choose to send or retain this letter.

Empathize: Remember when you needed another person's forgiveness, even if your infraction in this case was less damaging than your loved one's. If you can empathize with the other person, it will help you forgive.

Commit: Forgive sincerely and wholeheartedly, committing to not speak or wish hurt upon the forgiven, but rather strive to understand them.

Release: When and if negative feelings return, reapply the process of forgiveness and know—even if you do not feel positive or rewarded in the moment of forgiveness—that those unwanted feelings will eventually fade. Returning to forgiveness may be as simple as reminding yourself, "I forgive."

Recommitting Fully, Rebuilding Together

To feel like you are "all in," your relationship needs more than a verbal commitment. It demands consistent actions beyond words that address the infractions made. If you have been unfaithful, or if you have habitually put work, friends, and family of origin before your relationship, your mindset and attitude that led you to such behavior must be so radically altered as to be nonexistent.

A recommitment statement may be expressed in the singular, as in "I will." It can also be inclusive, signifying your decision to rebuild in partnership with your significant other.

Below are examples of affirmations you can adapt to your own recommitment promise:

- We will recognize and appreciate each other's abilities, unique strengths, and contributions and improvements to our relationship.
- We will communicate our hurts and worries instead of acting out irrationally.

- We will listen empathically and show compassion for each other.
- We will manage the stressors in our lives, self-regulate, have good boundaries, and put our relationship first.
- We will solve problems, grow from our mistakes, and make decisions together.

Reflection | Day 2: Finding Hope

Points to Remember

When two people want to reset their relationship, they need to practice thoughtful responses and deliberate actions that include apologizing sincerely, making amends, forgiving, recommitting fully, and rebuilding together. If your partner doesn't "hear" your apology, write a note, asking if you have missed something. Remind them that you are willing to do your part and need them to do theirs.

Questions to Consider

What has interfered with your reset in the past? Is it not providing a sincere apology, being unable to give true forgiveness, or being unable to fully recommit to the relationship?

Action Plan

Using the statements above as a sample, write your recommitment plan and keep it visible, revising as needed.

Day 3

Growth Mindset

Is this familiar?

You've been telling yourself, "This is all too hard. We've become so stuck in our routines and patterns, there's no way to work ourselves out of it. Our ways are set."

Day 3 will help you resolve defeatist feelings about your relationship and will help you find the strength to begin to do the work of building a lasting love.

A growth mindset in your relationship means you believe that with extra time and effort you can have a stronger relationship. In her aforementioned book, psychologist Carol Dweck points out that, after studying the behavior of thousands of children, she discovered some give up when a problem is too complex, while others find success by showing that they believe they can solve the problem before them by developing new skills.[1]

Recent advances in neuroscience also confirm that as you practice new habits and strategies, neural networks form new bonds that strengthen and promote them. The brain is waiting to give you a fresh start when you put in extra work. It seems that the well-worn statement, "I am stubborn, that's just not me, I couldn't do that," is just not true.

I admit that it takes work to change the habit of giving up too quickly. The inner voice of resistance is loudest when you prepare to do something beneficial and powerful. No one has heard this voice audibly, but all have experienced the fear and loss of energy after deciding to do something difficult. It may seem easier to be complacent and maintain the status quo, believing that the problem will solve itself, or that it's really just the other person's to solve.

I can guess that in some areas of your life you have said "no" to giving up and proven the success of hard work and relentless effort. If you have, consider if in these instances you were employing these recommended strategies, even if unknown to yourself at the time:

Being aware of your resistance. Notice your resistance to new habits, and how easily you return to old, comfortable, and disastrous behaviors.

Renewing your determination. Know that change will happen in everyone's life. Your decision to identify what and how you change gives you control of the outcome.

Applying a renewed effort. Persist with new words and actions, knowing that neural networks form new connections that support improvement and that your brain adapts to the new tasks you set, becoming more adept over time.

More than anything, a growth mindset requires you to cultivate a positive perspective and healthy optimism.

In kindergarten, many of us read the story about the little engine that thought it could. Charming in its simplicity, the story describes three engines asked, in turn, to pull an extremely heavy train over an unusually heavy grade in order to bring its goods to a destination. To paraphrase, the first engine is large and strong but hesitates, saying, "It is a very heavy train," and the second engine, also large, says, "It is a very heavy grade." The hero of the story is the small engine that replies, "I think I can."

A relationship of any length will face "heavy" circumstances at some point. It is at these moments that you may feel the least capable of producing a can-do attitude, when it is then that it is most needed. But at such times a growth mindset can ensure your awareness of your resistance, which can then promote a renewed determination and energy.

Let me describe a couple struggling in a fixed mindset that viewed their problems as overwhelming and impossible.

When I met Brian, he was so frustrated with Andrea that he couldn't find anything positive about her. He described her as perennially late, unreliable, and not pulling her weight. He admitted that his frustration had moved to contempt and criticism. He came to me asking what he should do. "I can't figure her out. *It shouldn't be this hard*," he said.

I could hear his pain. After all, the movies we love don't take us past happily ever after, and no one tells us that the real work starts after we cross the threshold of the front door and face a partner who is always late and unreliable.

Andrea didn't believe that Brian was swallowing this much distress nor that she was the cause. She admitted to resisting Brian's "structure, routine, and planned activities," preferring to be spontaneous. She felt strongly that adjusting to Brian was compromising her personality and she too felt that *a relationship shouldn't be this hard*.

"Let's play the game of the little engine that could," was my request to the couple as I handed them each paper and a pencil.

"If you were to succeed in pulling the relationship train and making it lighter for both of you, what could you change?"

I pointed out each partner's "fixed attitudes" in their relationship, but the real win was to hear Brian admit that Andrea was a lot of fun, and Andrea admit that Brian's structure allowed them to stay on track financially.

The reality is that, like Brian and Andrea, we must decide not only what we will change but how we will change it. How to do it begins with the energy of a positive mindset.

Building the Growth Mindset

We can be guilty of just "getting by" in our relationships, an attitude that does not foster connection, build trust, or enhance satisfaction. The following four recommendations help build relationships through utilizing a growth mindset and properly devoting real effort and time.

Build Friendship

What does it take for a couple to strengthen their friendship? Of course, trust, reliance, and availability are a good start. But how you invest extra time and effort will make a difference.

Be genuinely interested in your partner. What questions could you ask to have a complete picture of their past and present and understand them on a deeper level?

Tell me about your best friend in grade school.

How did you spend the summer holidays on the farm?

If you had a choice, where would you work?

Remember the details. Do you know their favourite color, drink, or musical group? Do you know where a mole, a scar, or a birthmark is? Ask and share equally.

Show genuine admiration and fondness. In the remake of the movie *A Star is Born,* country rock singer Jackson is shown watching songwriter Ally's performance with awe and wonder. This depiction reminds us how in those early days of romance, we can be just so impressed by our significant other. We beamed admiration for all they did, the significant or mundane, whether they were storytelling, entering a room, or making a meal. Our fondness was evident in our tone, questions, and smiles.

That same sense of wonder and awe are always at your fingertips to be reignited. In everyday or special occasions, show and tell your partner, "You're the best."

Acknowledgement and Appreciation

Failing to express "please" and "thank you," especially for what we consider "everyday" events, may be the primary cause of your partner's taken-for-granted mentality—but it need not stay that way. Level up your efforts by acknowledging your partner's assets and contributions in tangible ways. Give specific compliments that acknowledge their uniqueness and how they've improved your well-being. Write notes to them and prepare thoughtful gifts for them. Also, make more efforts to lighten their load with around-the-house duties and other obligations. Your partner may especially appreciate when technology-free time is devoted to them. With each gesture of acknowledgment and appreciation you will warm your partner's heart and help to build a stronger and stronger friendship.

Build Positive Memories

We cannot fully rely on those "big" life events for providing spaces to build positive memories with our partners, whether they be births, birthdays, graduations, holidays, or major vacations. It is up to us to actively build into our relationships as many other opportunities as possible to forge happy memories with our partners in moments dedicated to togetherness, even in the smallest of ways. When the fleeting joys of job promotions and new shiny cars recede, what we have left are the moments we make by the spaces we create for them. The fuller the reservoir of happy memories we can share with our partners, the more they will begin to feel like "home" in our hearts, further securing our intimate bonds.

Here are some examples of memory-making events that couples have shared with me:

Playing a sport together. The couple in mind forged a friendship at their local tennis club and now enjoy playing together.

Date night. One couple described the early years of watching pennies when they were unwilling to spend money on expensive dates. They now look forward to a tray of *hors d'oeuvres* and dessert every Friday night.

Exercise. Some couples schedule their workouts together, or deliberately engage in other healthy, physical activities together, like gardening or riding bikes. Sometimes they utilize such activity to provide each other mutual support and accountability. Many say that they feel a natural high and are more playful and flirtatious when engaged in various forms of exercise together. Others feel that their thoughts and emotions are more fluid and spontaneous during physical exercise in a way that promotes easier conversation.

Building and creating. One couple I know has built their furniture together. Another started a greeting card company. Another says that the idea for her landscaping business developed from the couple's love of outdoor work.

Games and puzzles. If you have spent time with family over monopoly, UNO, cards, Scattergories, or Scrabble, you know how fun and enjoyable games are.

Sometimes, creating positive memories with our partners doesn't require scheduling any event or activity at all, but merely being *present* with them at any given moment; such moments could be when we are their shoulder to cry on, when we are their hand to hold, or when we are their audience, ready to laugh at their corny joke.

Build on Opportunities

There are times when you are over the moon with joy, surrounded by ceremony, people, or crowds. You may have graduated, got a promotion, or won an award. At other times, you have lost someone, lost a position, lost hold of a dream, been disappointed in a friend or wounded by family. Sad, scared, guilty, or ashamed, you need and want a significant other to be physically present, hold you, and care for your practical and emotional needs. You want someone to listen and soothe, be compassionate and empathic, and keep you grounded. You need your significant other and no one else.

Whether it is us or our partners suffering in this way, these are all opportunities for us to make the effort to show our dedication to maintaining and building our relationship bond. Even a single missed opportunity in these cases can have a significant impact on the health of a relationship.

Show Practical Support

How many times can your significant other fail to show support before you say, "It's all up to me, I have to do it all, they are not here when it matters, I can't depend on them?" A growth mindset helps us focus and see opportunities to be responsible and take the initiative.

Consider the following scene:

At a large gathering of friends thrown together by a couple on a winter's night, someone knocks on the couple's door to report a horn blaring and lights flashing on a vehicle outside. The hostess, busy with last-minute prep, finds that her partner, even standing in vicinity of the door, shows no interest in answering it, so she goes to the door herself to receive the information. She then approaches her partner.

> **She:** (*With a concerned look in her eyes.*) Honey, there is a horn blaring. It must be one of our guests.
> **He:** (*Smiling, shrugging, and barely moving.*) Huh!

The woman then rolls her eyes and walks outside to take care of the incident.

If the woman's partner had answered the door and handled the incident himself, she would have silently said to herself, "I can count on him." Instead, she continues to believe, "I have to do it all."

If this pattern continues, her frustration and resentment will grow, and unconsciously she will label him negatively. He has neglected an opportunity.

Be Present When Your Partner Describes a Painful Past

"My mother didn't seem to know we were around. Our house was in chaos all the time. I never invited friends over."

When your significant other shares revealing details such as this, there is only one reasonable response: "I am so sorry this happened to you. It must have been awful."

Listening, asking questions, and having an appropriate tone and mode of expression all send a message that you care.

Be emotionally present when your partner reveals their personality quirks, vulnerabilities, hopes, and dreams. Notice and acknowledge weighty stories that make them tear up or cause a sudden shift in emotion. Whether significant or minute, when you are encouraging and treasure these moments, your significant other knows one thing: you are safe to be with.

Build Mind, Body, and Soul Connection

As life gets busier, there is less time for cuddling, reading to each other, or doing the activities that originally brought you together. So, there are fewer opportunities for couples to recreate the moments of exploring distant dreams and longings, aimless wandering, and meaningful touch. But it is true bonding and togetherness, whether in goofy playfulness or gazing at one another, that sustains a relationship of openness and reminds your significant other of your authentic self with which they once fell in love.

You don't have to be the same person you were before. You may have added new goals and want to pursue separate interests, but you won't have the strong relationship you previously did without bonding and connection. Share the responsibility for mind, body, and soul connection and take advantage of regular everyday events like a morning walk, an extra-long hug, cuddling, massaging each other, gazing into each other's eyes, and holding an embrace.

I must admit that many people feel awkward when they purposefully look into their partner's eyes. Like no other feature, eyes reflect your thoughts and emotions, taking your partner behind the scenes, and leaving you feeling more vulnerable.

To strengthen your bond with your partner, try the following exercises:

Gazing:
1. Sit facing each other as comfortably as possible.
2. Silently look into each other's eyes, being as composed as you can.
3. Try to sustain your shared gaze for at least five minutes.
4. Then tell each other how you feel.

Accept some discomfort, the desire to laugh and avoid the tension of an activity that leaves you feeling awkward. If your uneasiness or annoyance is excessive, appreciate that this exercise is especially beneficial to the longevity of your connection.

Holding:
1. Sit comfortably, embrace, and be as close as possible.
2. Rest your head into the other person's neck or shoulder.

3. Adjust yourself to avoid strain.
4. Tell each other how you feel.

Learning to Grow

As we have seen in the six relationship-growth-building recommendations, a little time and effort will make a big difference in addressing relationship problems. Greta and Bob provide a real-life example of a couple who went from a negative mindset about each other to a more understanding and compassionate one.

When Greta and Bob first came to see me, they described a cycle of fighting, silence, then politeness and making up.

"He doesn't understand me," was Greta's heartfelt cry, while Bob's major complaint was Greta's demands. The substance of their grievances was real, and each perspective begged compassion.

The couple was surprised when I asked if they had talked about their need to be understood and put some effort into giving instead of getting.

I explained how a growth mindset helps us appreciate how a little time and effort will make a big difference in relationship problems. Since most, if not all, couples' problems can be solved with communication and empathic listening, I gave Greta and Bob a homework assignment to reframe the following commonly used statements that begin in these ways:

- I give up . . .
- I can't figure her out . . .
- This won't work . . .
- I am not good at relationships . . .
- Our relationship will never change . . .

How many people do this homework set in therapy? Those with a growth mindset do make the time and effort and experience positive change, while those that ignore suggestions and strategies are unlikely to experience improvement. Greta and Bob reframed the following sentences as such:

- ~~I give up . . .~~ This is hard, but I have time for our relationship.
- ~~I can't figure her out . . .~~ I can understand her if I ask questions and listen carefully.
- ~~This won't work . . .~~ A good relationship takes time and patience.
- ~~I am not good at relationships . . .~~ Others have been successful and so can we.
- ~~Our relationship will never change . . .~~ When we address our faults and flaws, we can change.

Couples often become stuck in fixed mindsets in their relationships through negative thinking about each other, or one or the other believing they are always right and needing to win every argument. If this describes your relationship, talk to your partner about the trait or behavior you find irritating. Or reset your thinking with the help of the reflections below.

No One Is Perfect

Language is how we understand ourselves and others. Calling your significant other "selfish" or "lazy"—even just thinking of them in those term—is unhelpful.

Loser, *lazy*, or *crazy* are only a few of the painful barbs I have heard from couples. And each time I hear this, I also see a corresponding slump in the receiver's eyes and body, as if they've been slapped across the face. I fear that partners don't recover quickly from these "word wounds." Even if your partner acts like a crazy or lazy loser, use kind words to address their actions and explain how it affects you.

If you catch yourself elaborating on your partner's failings, remind yourself that everyone has their faults, that we all make mistakes and experience some failures. I remember the character of Harvey Dent, played by actor Aaron Eckhart, in the movie *The Dark Knight*, saying, "You either die a hero, or you live long enough to see yourself become the villain."

Believing You Are Always Right

Imagine how deflating it is for your significant other to face the same brick wall of resistance to their opinions and ideas over and over, only hearing, "Take it or leave it," and, "I don't care." When this ultimatum is present, the partnership is lost; one person loses interest and the other loses significant companionship.

When the either/or perspective prevails in a couple's relationship, the one who "loses" feels insignificant and misunderstood. In fact, one way to monitor a growth mindset in a relationship is through an individual willingness to listen, brainstorm, and explore your partner's ideas. The model of win-win, where both parties are heard, validated, and accommodated, is the growth perspective that promotes true partnership.

The little engine with its train never let go of its growth mindset, and as it went along the rails it kept repeating to itself, "I think I can. I think I can. I think I can."

As the journey intensified and it rolled toward the ascent, it kept repeating to itself: "I— think—I think I can. I—think—I can. I—think— I can."

Then it reached the grade, but its voice could still be heard: "I think I can. I . . . think . . . I . . . can. I . . . think . . . I . . . can." Higher and higher it climbed, and its voice grew fainter, and its words came slower: "I . . . . think . . . . I . . . . can."

It was almost to the top.

"I . . . . think . . ."

It was at the top.

"I . . . . can."

It passed over the top of the hill and began crawling down the opposite slope.

"I . . . think . . . I . . . can . . . I . . . thought . . . I . . . could. I . . . thought . . . I . . . could. I thought I could. I thought I could. I thought I could."

And singing its triumph, it rushed on down toward the valley.

Relationship happiness always hinges on the effort you make—an effort worthwhile because you have not only grown, but have done so together with your partner. You have become more resilient, more emotionally intelligent. You manage stress better than before and have gained the confidence in knowing you are the key to your own success. You learn, as Brian and Andrea did, that frustrations, criticism, and contempt have no place in your life; and like Greta and Bob, you have become more compassionate and selfless.

Reflection | Day 3: Growth Mindset

Points to Remember
Devoting real time and effort will make a significant difference in the quality of your relationship.

Questions to Consider
To what area of your life have you devoted the most time and energy? Can you connect your effort to actual rewards?

Action Plan
To increase love and appreciation for your partner, start listing their assets and contributions as often as they appear. After a week of reading these, notice how your attitude has shifted. Do you want to go deeper? Journal about your observations, share with your partner what you've noticed about them, and consider how you feel afterward. Here are some examples of journal entries you could make:

- It's nice to have someone bring me coffee in bed. I feel special and want to do something for them.
- I complain that he doesn't help around the house, but last week when I listed what he did, I discovered that he makes a fair contribution.
- When I started noticing her smile and what she does with her eyes, I was more attracted.

We remember what we focus on.

You can go deeper still and create gratitude cards for your significant other, writing on each one thing you are thankful for about them. Continue to share your positive appreciation and invite your partner to play the "Little Engine That Could" game with you.

Responding to Signals for Attention

Is this familiar?

"My partner doesn't see me," you've heard yourself thinking. "It doesn't feel like they're here with me. I feel so lonely in this relationship."

I am concerned that even well-meaning partners fail their relationship by being passive and unconsciously neglectful. Day 4 will help you understand why partners do not give one another the attention they need and deserve, and will provide communication strategies to help you repair your connection.

I am an introvert, guilty of being so absorbed in my own thoughts that I neglect my surroundings, catching my husband's comments only on the second time around. I have a memory of one evening when he was sitting across from me reading a magazine and chuckling, and five minutes later he was full-on laughing. Finally, he left the room with a disappointed look. When I asked him what's wrong, he said, "You didn't hear me, see me, or ask me what was funny." That was the catalyst for my becoming a more responsive partner.

John Gottman, an American psychologist who has done extensive research with couples for more than four decades, says that a couple makes a "bid" for each other's attention every day.[1] In an evening together, they will try to impress, connect, and engage up to one hundred times. Whether your significant other glances in your direction, says something about the weather, you, the home, the children, or the news, they want you to look at them, reply, and show interest. The ploy may be subtle or mundane, the topic dull or riveting; your partner wants your attention every day. They are unconsciously saying, "I want you to see me. I want to feel your presence. Answer my questions by touching, smiling, and walking over to me. Anything. But please respond." Attention is your way of affirming a connection, and your preoccupation elsewhere breaks the bond. Consider three possible responses to your significant other's signal:

1. Hostility and disagreement. (Walking away.)
2. Preoccupation and disengagement. (Standing still.)
3. Engagement and enthusiasm. (Walking toward the signal with open arms.)

Which of these responses leave the other person confused and hurt, which angry and hostile, and which believing that they matter and assures them that you will remain close? This question seems to have an easy answer, but it's not an easy problem.

Your relationship goal is for each partner to *walk toward* one another's signals for care and attention. For now, let's examine what it means to "stand still" and to "walk away."

"Standing still" is a metaphor for a person being unresponsive, noncommittal, and overall disinterested with their partner. When your significant other believes they are insignificant to you, they believe they are inadequate, show their hurt by expressing anger, withdrawing, or even resorting to a show of similar disinterest. They may even begin drifting toward others who fill that void. Regardless of the degree of "standing still," the result is a breach in closeness.

"Walking away" is a metaphor that describes the chain reaction of cold, distant, and harsh interactions between partners that indicates an increasingly broken connection. During a time of "walking away," the negativity that each partner feels toward the other makes it impossible to ignore the "everyday" offenses and frustrations like crumbs on the kitchen counter, forgotten items on a grocery list, or the smell of burnt toast, the way you did before.

Walking Away or Standing Still

Your attention to your significant other is the secret to your connection. Your partner sends deliberate or unconscious signals for attention—a glance, a raised brow, a look, a touch on your shoulder, a question, a comment, even an accidental bump against your hip. When they are frustrated by your lack of response, the tone of the signal can range from outright begging for your time and finding excuses to be around you, to being hurt and downright nasty. In this latter state, your significant other picks fights, is passive-aggressive, undermines you, stops sharing their needs, and withdraws and avoids intimacy. This cycle of reactivity must be avoided as it gradually crushes the soul of the relationship and the people in it. If the connection continues to slide, a partner may be left open and vulnerable to the attention and emotional connection of another—your relationship, once imbued with "magic," once cheat-proof, now has chinks.

To be fair, most of us can't imagine ignoring our loved ones, but we may suddenly find ourselves faced with feeling that we have no alternative. Events such as the birth of children, the demands of another friend's or family member's disability, the call of aging parents, your own desire to get ahead, or social pressure to join a group all demand our immediate attention and energy, and we may be inclined to place a significant other on hold. We expect them to understand why we are distracted and continue to nurture us, but we may only find diminishing returns.

The Marriage Checkup study, conducted by a team at Clark University, identified busyness as one of the most common reasons that couples don't give each other needed attention.[2] The real tasks of life—commuting, driving our children to dance classes and hockey practice, and buying groceries for Mom and Dad—all use the time we might otherwise spend giving attention.

Tasked in so many directions, we crave time alone, time to unwind, time to socialize with others, time to create. Hence, we go to bed later and linger apart from our spouses in order to breathe, relax, and replenish on our own.

If we hope to save our relationships, one partner needs to be aware and take action. If it is the partner who feels lonely, they can say so and ask for what they need in positive, non-accusatory terms. Yet this rarely happens. Instead, once-loving partners often default to protesting with complaints, criticism, and withdrawal. They "diagnose" the issue from within, seeing only a single-sided view, and use indirect, circuitous modes of communication—and rarely ever say, "I love you and miss you."

The Why Behind Walking Away or Standing Still

It is healthy to want your partner's attention; such a desire is, in fact, vital to your connection. Without positive attention, couples are roommates living parallel lives who end up walking away or standing still.

The following are possible factors that may be catalysts for a partner's "walking away" and "standing still" responses:

- Personality
- Attachment theory
- Mindlessness
- Work-life imbalance
- Poor role models

Personality

Personality plays a crucial role in your interactions with a significant other. For example, introverts may be less expressive, seem less responsive and engaged, and need more time alone. On the other hand, extroverts are more demonstrative, seek out opportunities to touch and talk, and are quick to detect your signals for attention.

If your partner seems to fall into the introvert category, seeming less engaged than you are, make your observation known to them in the spirit of understanding. Personality differences are not generally an issue for couples who are patient, aware, sensitive to each other's needs, and committed to being together.

Attachment Theory

Not only are we all born with glorious differences in DNA that produce all of our various personality types, but our diverse childhood experiences also impact the way we form relationships in adulthood. The research that supports this concept was first developed in the 1950s by British psychiatrist and psychoanalyst John Bowlby, resulting in what is now well known as "attachment theory."

Attachment theory says that we develop as secure beings when we are consistently loved and cared for, and in turn we learn healthy dependence on others. As a secure child we grow up to ask for what we need and are more likely to manage the fluctuations in future relationships. Secure individuals give attention freely and prompt others to give them attention when it is lacking. By contrast, the child with insecure attachment experiences may be either anxious, avoidant, or disorganized, coping poorly when later faced with inadequate attention from a spouse. The anxiously attached partner may be clingy, feeling unworthy of love; the partner with a disorganized attachment style can exhibit confusing relationship behaviors such as chronic anxiety and a proclivity toward avoidance.

You may be thinking that the strongest likelihood of finding a responsive partner is to seek a partner who is not only securely attached but has a similar personality type as you. This may be so except when nature serendipitously seeks to pair us as complements to each other.

Mindlessness

A partner's seemingly disrespectful responses of "walking away" or "standing still" may not always be an indication of their ill will or meanness. Sometimes, their inability to respond positively to the other is unconscious behavior caused by their own ignorance of how essential effortful bonding is to any relationship.

A partner's seemingly mindless attitude and dismissive body language may also be misdirected reflexes resulting from their own anger and hurt.

Imbalance of Work and Relationship Play

A busy couple who are not as engaged and attentive to one another as when they first met is by default saying, "Our relationship can wait until we have more time and money, and when our children are grown and there are fewer demands." Because relationships are organic and develop naturally over time, without force or planning, it can only ever be the present moment, the present experience, that shapes it. Like a plant that won't survive without water, sunshine, air, and special care, inattention starves a relationship, but applying constant, committed attention will preserve it.

Poor Role Models

Our partners may have grown up in homes where their parents were uncomfortable with showing emotion or distracted or burdened by too many responsibilities to show proper attention and care, resulting in their own inability to be fully responsive in a relationship. Such a partner may not be paying close enough attention, and thus not responding promptly, to our subtle advances. If your partner doesn't see that you want their attention, tell them you do, and offer a safe forum for them to discuss with you why they are detached.

Ultimately, when your significant other ignores or responds negatively toward your signals for attention, your relationship is at risk—your desire to be seen, heard, and highly regarded by this special person is so consequential that you cannot bear to be "invisible." Some who experience disengagement in a relationship are vulnerable to seeking out the connection they need and can drift between relationships to enjoy a "honeymoon," again and again. Others redirect their energy to something that won't disappoint—a game, pet, hobby, work, or achievement. Still, others choose to continue on in a relationship where they accept disconnection and lead parallel lives.

Opening Your Arms

A core ingredient of connection is responsiveness, but the partner feeling lonely in a relationship has a part to play in restoring the connection. This part requires speaking up without complaint and criticism, and resisting the temptation of withdrawing into silence or distraction.

Marcie and Alan were one couple who moved from distance to engagement.

They were drifting away from engagement for all the reasons listed above: personality differences, insecurity, mindlessness, work-life imbalances, and even childhood role models who were neglectful or obsessive of their partners. Together for six years and married for three, they were a perfect match on paper, with similar interests, a community of friends, the same conservative family values, and a love of adventure and learning. What could go wrong?

Marcie claimed to be satisfied with her life with Alan, but Alan complained that she was distracted, always working, spending all of her free time talking to friends, and close to some device the rest of the time. She had good explanations for her activities: she needed to network in order to build her business, and she was confused as Alan had originally encouraged her in this adventure. Marcie agreed to put a limit on her workday and spend less time on devices, but was inconsistent, soon defaulting to her busyness.

Alan responded with the silent treatment, punishing her by refusing to participate in Marcie's journey. Meanwhile, Marcie explained that when Alan showed anger and vengefulness she wanted to be as far away from him as possible. To this Alan was shocked, not understanding why Marcie focused on his anger and not his desire to be with her. He was hurt that she didn't want to be with him as much as he wanted to be with her.

Alan didn't want just any kind of attention. He saw Marcie dispensing a sort of generally pleasant attention to family friends, to neighbors, and even to the cashier at the grocery store, understanding that this was in her nature. But her time with him could only be read as "distracted attention" that told Alan, "You are unimportant."

The need for proximity to a loved one and attention from them is hardwired in most of us, evident to anyone who watches an infant's eyes following a parent and responding to their movements, sounds, and touches. Later, as the little one grows, they become more selective, picking that "special person" out in a room, perhaps looking at others too, but returning to the "one" over and over again—the caregiver, likely the mother. Decades later, the grown man or woman bonds in a romantic relationship by instinctively seeking the warmth and the attention they hopefully received in their childhood, attention that confirmed they were safe and secure, and that all was well with the world.

Nothing changed for Marcie and Alan until they embraced the reality that their life together was the highest priority, and Alan changed his responses to Marcie to be more empathic and understanding. I was tempted to tell Marcie, "Just do it. When you said, 'I do,' you're contracted to give attention." But I was certain without mutual understanding and a shift in perspective, the couple was doomed to disconnection.

Marcie and Alan, with their personality differences, insecurity, mindlessness, work-life imbalances, and poor childhood role models, needed to be conscious and intentional about attention. They ultimately recognized their mutual distress, accepted their relationship needs, and were prepared to gift each other with undivided attention. They also learned how easy it would be for them to revert to the pattern they existed in for so many years. She was driven and distracted, and he was hurt and withdrawn. So, they carved out generous and specific times for togetherness.

Below is the empathy-listening exercise that helped them understand each other's very different needs and personalities.

> *"Attention is the most basic form of love.*
> *Through it, we bless and are blessed."*
> —Attributed to Zen Teacher John Tarrant

Conscious and Continuous

I aided Marcie and Alan with an empathy-listening exercise that helped them to understand each other's needs and different personalities. For them this exercise included conscientious actions, such as walking outside together in the morning and physically greeting and touching when someone arrived home. Meanwhile, Marcie implemented clear and consistent boundaries around her workday, while Alan agreed that his silent treatment was out of bounds. The couple wrote out their vision of relationship togetherness and transcribed it as wall art.

We walk together every day.
We clean and cook together.
We reply to each other's texts right away.
We don't accept projects that involve evenings and weekends.

Marcie confessed to being grateful for the changes soon after the couple put some boundaries in place and said, without Alan's protest, that she was heading for burnout. The couple decided to reboot with a vacation.

Empathy Listening Exercise

Empathy is emptying our heart and mind to walk in another's shoes.

How to perform the empathy-listening exercise:

1. *Establish the setting for listening.* Sit with your partner with a clear, empty glass pitcher on the table between you as a reminder to listen "empty." On alternate days, you will speak for twenty minutes while the other practices listening and reflecting with the following four principles in mind:
    - Do not express your opinion, and make an effort not to judge.
    - Identify with the other person's feelings through your open expressions.

- Briefly and thoughtfully summarize what your partner has told you.
- Openly acknowledge your partner's feelings.

2. *Listen patiently*. When listening to another person during a conversation, we find it difficult to wait before starting to talk about our own interests. Practice these techniques:
   - Take a breath, breathe out distractions, and refocus your attention.
   - Slow down and pay attention.
   - Nurture curiosity. Trust that listening will take you somewhere interesting.
   - Set aside your impulse to say anything.

3. *Interrupt your exercises productively*. As with any exercise, there are exceptions. Question the speaker if something is not clear. Answer a question the speaker asks you.

Once you understand each other's responses, like Marcie and Alan came to do, you can make a conscious effort to change your behaviors.

Walk Toward Your Partner's Signal

When we notice our partner's expressions, when we conscientiously answer their questions, when we honestly inquire about their feelings and thoughts, and when we show a genuine interest in their dreams and desires, our emotional connection is preserved. There is the feeling again of being "in a relationship." Once there, partners feel capable of overlooking each other's mistakes, seeing the other's point of view, collaborating and coming to agreement, and celebrating the relationship without resistance.

> *"We cannot let another person into our hearts or minds unless we empty ourselves. We can truly listen to him or truly hear her only out of emptiness."*
> —Attributed to Psychiatrist M. Scott Peck

Walking Away, Standing Still, and Walking Toward Responses

Call for Attention	Walking Away (Hostility and Disagreement)	Standing Still (Preoccupation and Disengagement)	Walking Toward (Engagement and Enthusiasm)
Honey, I'm home!	So?	I need help with supper.	Great! You beat the traffic. Let me help you with your things. Help me with dinner after?
What's on the agenda tonight?	Dinner, dishes, same old! Nothing that concerns you.	Did you pay the telephone bill?	I'm looking forward to a quiet evening. Would you like to team up on chores and bills and then decide what you'd like to do?
Did you read about what happened today in the news?	Please be quiet. I'm trying to concentrate.	(No response.)	No, I didn't! Please tell me about it.
This is a great art exhibit!	I don't see what you see in any of this.	Are you ready to go?	What have been your favorite pieces so far?

Reflection | Day 4:
Responding to Signals for Attention

Points to Remember
You feel connected when your arms are open and you are walking "toward" your significant other.

Questions to Consider
How would your relationship change if you were more responsive to your partner? What can you do to reinforce a responsive style of communication?

Action Plan
With kindness, tell your partner when and how they are being unresponsive. Consider if there is a reason for their being unresponsive. Share your thoughts with your significant other and renew your commitment to "walk toward." Meanwhile, let your partner know when you notice their efforts to be engaged by showing your warmth and appreciation.

Making a Match of Different Personalities

Is this familiar?

"We are just so different," you've begun to think. "Maybe we weren't meant to be together . . ."

Day 5 will help you to see your personality differences with your partner in a new light.

What happens when you become annoyed and frustrated at the same characteristics you appreciated in your partner when you were newly in love?

It appears that we can be equally satisfied in a relationship with someone of a similar personality as one who is different, even if a successful relationship requires trial and error through continual effort. One study conducted by Michigan State University researchers concluded that similarity in personality does not predict compatibility.[1] In addition, psychologist Amanda Glynn writes that although people gravitate toward those more like them, the research does not prove they are more compatible.[2]

You are attracted to romantic partners not only by personality traits you share with them, but also by ones you do not possess yourself.

Throughout a lifetime, couples can sharpen and relax each other's traits in many helpful ways.

Nature favors differentiation. You may have many things in common with your partner, but just as no two sunrises, snowflakes, or leaves of a tree are identical, you are also different from your partner in key ways. You grew up in different homes and in different circumstances, whether culturally or socioeconomically. Your family is distinct from any other, as is your DNA. When one person says, "We need to talk," it may be an invitation to solve a problem, while the other may consider the statement to be threatening. "Let's go for a walk," means a strenuous hike for one but a relaxed, romantic stroll for another. Make your relationship fair and equitable, instill a value for individual differences and stand up for them.

Couples can adjust to diversity in personality style by respecting boundaries, requesting behavior change as needed, making other simple tweaks, and, especially, celebrating differences.

(Disclaimer: If your significant other uses their personality as an excuse for violence or abuse, the following suggestions do not apply.)

Respect Each Other's Boundaries

Boundaries define who we are. Essential to our happiness, they describe our limitations and our guidelines based on our values, desires, and goals. Like drawing a personal property line that marks what you are responsible for, communicating your boundaries clearly and caringly is your responsibility to your partner, as is getting to know their own boundaries. In this we may reduce incidents of trespassing, honest or dishonest misunderstandings, disrespect of needs and preferences, entitlement, and bullying.

Healthy boundaries promote the individual freedom of each partner, guiding the relationship like a charter of rights. Declarations of healthy boundaries may be:

- I can explore my preferences and still be loved.
- I can say no without losing your love.

- I can love you and disagree with you.
- I can be myself.

If you are in a relationship where you do not feel you can make such declarations, there are actions you can take to begin repairing boundaries and rebuilding your bond with your partner.

Request Behavior Change

Let's face it, even with the best boundaries or intentions, two people sharing their lives together will irritate and frustrate each other at times. Asking for reasonable change is not a rejection of your significant other's personality, but a fair and healthy way to address their behavior that is causing distress. Just keep your tone undemanding, limit your expectations, and be specific.

Type A–Type B | Extrovert–Introvert

Adjusting to personality differences may require nothing more than a few minor tweaks. First, let's look at the common personality differences—and thus competing expectations of boundaries—that couples face. Personalities can generally be divided into groupings: type A and type B, and extroverts and introverts. A type A personality can actually be an introvert, and a type B can even be an extrovert. The difference is that type As can be especially driven, ambitious, status-conscious, and even rigidly organized, impatient, and at times aggressive. They prefer to deal with issues promptly. Type Bs, on the other hand, are often less competitive and can show more tolerance in the face of problems. They take a more laid-back approach to their lives, preferring to address problems incrementally.

Meanwhile, extroverts are centered externally, gaining energy from being around others and preferring to solve problems by talking about them openly. They simply *thrive* around other people. Introverted personalities are internally centered, however, rejuvenating best in solitude and preferring to take substantial time to work out problems in their own minds. They thrive in their own independence.

When relationships consist of a type A–type B pairing, various problems may arise and may be further complicated by an extrovert–introvert clash. Type A partners might find themselves simply dissatisfied with the personality of their type B partner, disappointed by their seeming lack of drive—leaving the type B partner feeling as if they cannot please their type A partner in a consistent way, resulting in their feeling stuck in a cycle of failure, causing them low self-esteem.

In craving company, the extrovert may become bored or impatient with their introverted partners and dissatisfied with their relationship. Conversely, the introvert might find their extroverted partner too demanding, leaving them feeling depleted and without enough time to unwind and feel restored.

The problems that may arise between partners in a type A–type B or extrovert–introvert pairing can very well be "tweaked" into harmony. Consider the following strategies for smoothing out type A–type B and extrovert–introvert friction.

Type A Tweaks to Avoid Problems with a B Partner

Perhaps the greatest challenge for a type A personality with a type B partner is understanding that a type B person can achieve the same level of personal and professional success in life even at their more measured pace; that speed and intensity is not always correlated with drive; and especially that their partner cares just as much as they do about their relationship but just shows it in a different way. Type As should find, however, that being open to making slight adjustments for their type B partner will only work to enhance their bond with their type B partner.

Recognize the Need for Personal Change

When you notice the negative effect of your type A characteristics on your partner's well-being, try not to ignore the signs but begin to seek a middle path that reduces stress and improves harmony in the relationship. If this leads you to release control and opt for a more relaxed personality style, you are on the right path. Continue to monitor that path, focusing on process and not solely on outcomes so you can appreciate your life together.

Practice Stress Management

Deep-breathing techniques can help calm the mind when you feel stress or impatience building. Along with a regular practice of mindfulness and meditation, deep breathing can also help slow down your thoughts, reduce stress, and encourage a more relaxed approach to life.

Prioritize Balance

Honor your type B partner's devotion to finding work/life balance by scheduling leisure, relaxation, hobbies, and socializing into your weekly agenda. Delegating tasks and trusting others to handle responsibilities also helps you maintain a healthy balance.

Form Healthier Habits.

Even the productivity gurus admit that working quickly and multitasking is an ineffective work/life strategy. So consider pacing yourself in daily activities to enjoy your type B partner who may already be walking and driving more slowly or savoring conversations that don't rush to conclusions. As you listen more, practice teamwork and cooperation, your partner has more space to shine.

Type-B Tweaks to Avoid Problems with an A Partner

Type Bs with type A partners are challenged with the task of finding equal footing with a person whose energy and drive can feel overpowering at times and discourage full participation in their relationship, whether it comes to problem-solving or activities. The more a type B takes the brave step to stake their own claim in their relationship, however, the more their type A partner will recognize how much stronger it makes their bond.

Initiate Conversations

Type B personalities naturally have a more challenging time voicing their feelings and concerns with their type A partner, but it is still incumbent upon a B to find the courage to initiate conversations and remain tactful in their approach, including nonjudgmentally and patiently listening to their A partner. As the conversation begins, it is equally important for a B personality to acknowledge their A partner's needs and make an effort to work in tandem—not by themselves in their own mind—to develop a plan *together* that is reciprocally accommodating.

Check In Regularly

As you continue to build the courage as a type B person to initiate discussions about your feelings, needs, and preferences, making such discussions a regular occurrence will continually help to reduce misunderstandings and ensure that you remain on the same page.

Keep a Positive Mindset

When you frame your partner's drive and methods of organization positively, you will see that they complement your calmness and adaptability. From there you can both recognize that it is by working *together* that you can make more well-rounded decisions and share a vision. Conversations that acknowledge differences and reframe them as strengths rather than obstacles will help you navigate relationship differences.

Remember Boundaries

Establish boundaries to ensure that your partner's personality does not overwhelm yours. For example, if your partner tends to push for quick decisions, you might agree on times when you both can take a step back and think things through.

Negotiate and Compromise

A special challenge for the type B personality is to avoid saying yes to escape conflict. Taking advantage of your natural type B ability to remain calm and de-escalate conflicts will help balance your partner's assertiveness and prevent arguments from getting out of control. Having said this, every relationship needs to resolve serious issues, so request time to think through both of your needs before making a compromise.

Avoid Passive Behavior

Make sure that your laid-back nature does not cause you to be passive in important matters. It's essential to express your opinions and preferences clearly, even if they differ from your partner's. Accept that not every disagreement needs to be resolved. Sometimes, it's okay to agree to disagree and move on, respecting each other's perspectives.

Promote Shared Goals and Interests

It is easy for couples in a relationship to overly focus on differences rather than activities that are equally enjoyed and goals that are equally shared. Prioritizing the latter will help strengthen your bond and allow both personalities to contribute to the relationship in meaningful ways.

Support Your Partner's Type-A Needs

In some ways your partner will see value in retraining certain aspects of their personality style, but where they don't you must remain supportive. They may need to practice organization and set structure in ways that you don't, but it is important to remember that balancing your own traits with their own will create relationship harmony. Furthermore, your type A partner will feel a deepened bond as they recognize your acceptance of their unique traits.

Balance Your Energies

In certain situations your partner may live at a faster pace and act with more urgency than you do. The key is to accept and gracefully meet your partner at your own pace so that you may both give and take in equal measure. Pay attention to when you need to "clear the path" for your partner, and where there's room to share it. In doing so, you will notice each other's differences less.

Maintain Your Identity

If you attempt to overly please a partner and adjust too radically to their personality, it can leave you wondering, "Who am I?" Protect your identity by continuing to engage in activities you enjoy with your friends and family and do not compromise on your core perspectives. This will only help you share a harmonious relationship balance with your partner.

If you are a type B and find these suggestions intimidating, just remember that relationship adjustments can be made incrementally over time as both you and your partner evolve.

Extrovert Tweaks to Avoid Problems with an Introverted Partner

Many of the strategies that a type A person uses to adjust to their type B partner will apply to the extrovert–introvert relationship, but since there are many extroverts who are type B and introverts who are type A, it will be helpful to list the major tweaks of understanding, respecting, and balancing their different social needs and energy levels.

Don't Pressure Socialization

Being introverted doesn't mean your partner is antisocial; they simply recharge in quieter, more solitary settings. Even at home, your significant other will want some alone time, so don't pressure them into engagement until they are ready. This is also true for social situations that may feel draining to your introvert partner. Many introverts work harder to fit in and belong, so accepting and appreciating the challenges your partner has when socializing for long periods will only draw you closer.

Open Dialogue and Clear Expectations

Discussing each other's social needs productively means that you conscientiously explain why you enjoy socializing and sincerely seek to understand why your partner values quiet time. Achieving this mutual understanding will greatly prevent misunderstandings. All the while, don't make assumptions about what your partner wants; before making plans, check in with them to ensure they're comfortable with your arrangements. Also make sure to set expectations about how often you'll engage in social activities together versus spending time apart.

Balance Social Activities and Time Together

Thoughtfully discuss the degree to which you and your partner will engage in any social event together. For example, if you want to attend a party, agree on the length of time you'll stay, or even offer your partner the option to skip the event if they show disinterest. Understand that it's okay to attend some social events alone. This allows you to fulfill your socializing needs without overwhelming your partner. During busy seasons, try to introduce a blend of small gatherings and quiet outings to help your significant other recharge.

Communicate Adaptively

Introverts need more time to process their thoughts before discussing issues. When you are patient and allow your introverted partner space and time to express themselves, you are likely to enjoy better conversations. Introversion shows itself in degrees, so not all introverts are the same. Generally speaking, an introverted partner doesn't enjoy excessive stimulation, so keeping your voice and tone subdued and dedicating extra attention to listening will only reduce the possibility of conflict with your loved one.

Engage in Introvert-Respectful Quality Time

Making space for meaningful, introvert-aligned interactions such as relaxed one-on-one conversations and other calm activities, such as peaceful walks, working on puzzles, or reading together, will strengthen your emotional connection to your partner and help ensure they can remain energized and focused in your presence.

Tweaks to Help an Introvert Avoid Problems with an Extroverted Partner

An introverted partner can thrive in a relationship with an extrovert by understanding and balancing their own needs with the social and energetic nature of their extroverted partner. Here are strategies to help an introvert navigate and enhance their relationship with an extrovert.

Respecting Differences

The gift that your extroverted partner hopes to receive is some freedom to go out and enjoy social activities, even if you don't always join them. This allows them to fulfill their needs without pressuring or judging you. Having said that, it is vital that you attend activities that matter to them. Activities such as graduations, weddings, and family events will etch a permanent memory on their heart, so be sure to show up for these big events.

Balance Your Needs with Personal Growth

While it is wise to exercise discretion as to what degree you choose to step outside of your comfort zones when it comes to socializing, try to use your relationship as a foundation to gain new social skills from your extroverted partner. Stepping out of your comfort zone periodically will not only nourish your relationship but will help you grow as individual. You may even find that over time you enjoy certain social activities more than you expected.

Communicate Social Comfort

Even when "stretching your legs" in socializing, being open and agreeing on your comfort levels with your partner in social settings is paramount. For example, at larger social events where you are a stranger you may ask to stick close to your partner or bring a friend who makes you feel at ease. Meanwhile, continue to choose social events with which you're reasonably comfortable attending. Be clear with your partner about which events you'll attend and which you might skip, without feeling guilty.

Avoid Becoming Overwhelmed

Set boundaries and continue to educate your partner on how you function best so they understand why you might take a sufficient pause before speaking, require shorter conversations, ask for a timeout to think things through, need more time to de-stress, etc. Remember that the overarching goal is for you and your partner to combine and mutually adapt to your personality differences for the sake of building a deeper understanding of one another that will strengthen your bond and promote harmonious partnership even in the most challenging conditions.

Always Celebrate Your Differences

To celebrate your partner's personality is to embrace and accept, not merely to tolerate. It is too easy to get used to a partner, believe you are better or more intelligent, default to criticism, and neglect to honor their efforts, praise their accomplishments, or notice their improvements. Your partner's personality deserves to be acknowledged, appreciated, and celebrated.

Eric and Eloise are an example of a couple suffering from personality differences and boundarylessness. They fell in love during their second year at university. They had different backgrounds, but after a short breakup, they married. Along the way, Eric adjusted to Eloise's exuberance, as well as her no-nonsense decision-making and firmly established expectations. Unfortunately, Eloise ultimately forgot to consider Eric's own preferences. Truth is, he admired Eloise, and the couple, at least initially, benefitted from her sound judgment.

Twenty years later, they were shocked when friends assumed they were happy. Both separately felt unappreciated, and their communication had suffered. They decided to seek counseling, and in their first round of appointments, Eloise told the therapist that they indeed talked a lot as a couple—but further probing revealed Eric's fear of speaking up and facing confrontation, admissions that led to revealing Eloise's subtle way of making Eric drop the subject in such a conversation. Eric resented the many ways his life had changed, the hobbies and interests he discarded, and the friends who no longer came around.

Eloise was also unhappy in her role of family manager and over-giver and wondered where she went wrong.

Eric and Eloise's second counseling experience was more productive: Eloise was ready to accept that some aspects of her personality made life intolerable for everyone, especially her. She began to make productive adjustments by no longer stringently defending her dream of "the perfect life." Eric himself was quick to take responsibility for reluctance to communicate his needs, while also equally quick to reassure Eloise about her crucial role in maintaining their family's stability.

The counselor explained to the couple how their individual personalities without boundaries created a life where neither heard the other saying "no," and each had trouble saying "no" to others. This revelation resonated when she described how Eloise experienced rigid limits and mimicked her parent's behavior, while Eric learned to help his single mother out by "fading" into the background. Eloise again saw herself as the five- and ten-year-old escaping to her room to avoid her father's alcoholic anger and believing "the world is not safe; I have no control."

The couple spent some time grieving, but learned that boundaries in all their relationships would help them navigate personality differences and heal personally. The counselor provided the couple with a playbook to help them along the way.

Playbook of Healthy Boundaries

Rule #1: Respect that we are all individuals separate from others. This means you shouldn't try to impose your personality, preferences, character, and choices on your partner or anyone else, including parents, siblings, friends, or even your children—especially adolescent or adult children! You are not responsible for managing their characteristics, but must instead respect and celebrate their differences. Notice their defensive reaction or outburst when you "tell" them what to do. Notice how you yourself bristle when someone orders or forces their opinion and preferences on you. With the exception of small children, power of attorney, or immediate crisis, the solution is to make your own decisions and respect that of others.

Rule #2: Let others be responsible for their own needs and desires. Do you have a tendency to try to solve your partner's problems, to have a solution before the other person recognizes the problem and rescues it themselves? Be responsible *to* others and not for others. Ask permission before offering advice or a solution.

Rule #3: Address issues when they come up. Notice any tendency to avoid topics of disagreement, or subjects you are self-conscious or anxious about. Notice your partner's body language and facial expressions and respond as if they are words. Risk some disagreement.

Rule #4: Accept that guilt, shame, and fear are part of speaking up. These emotions can bring a range of symptoms that are so uncomfortable you want nothing more than to escape. It may be a heart that is pounding, sweat beading on your forehead, tightness in your throat, a fuzzy lack of focus, and even panic. You may freeze up or want to lash out angrily. Just remind yourself: "I won't die; this feeling won't last." Wait for the emotions to subside or learn to distract yourself. Feel the fear and do it anyway.

Rule # 5: Remember that we all need others in our lives. Boundaries are not an excuse to isolate and exclude. Boundaries are not meant to keep others away, keep you distant and unavailable, or promote separation in general. They are there to help you gain freedom and strength to better serve. They are meant to encourage connectedness in both casual and intimate relationships. Boundaries are *reasonable* rules and expectations based on our mutual respect, kindness, and care for one another. When we learn to honor love and protect ourselves, we are better able to do the same for others.

Properly established and understood boundaries won't solve every problem a couple is having due to personality differences, but they create a solid foundation from which to begin to build a happier, mutually respectful relationship.

Reflection | Day 5:
Making a Match of Different Personalities

Points to Remember
When partners acknowledge, celebrate, and accommodate for each other's personality differences, they will be drawn closer together.

Questions to Consider
Do your boundaries promote your authenticity, enhance your wellness, and draw you closer to your partner?

Or do they confine you and create distance from them?

Action Plan
List 2–3 of your partner's personality traits and describe how they have impacted you positively.

Next, identify 2–3 of your partner's personality traits or behaviors that you wish were different. Releasing any expectation of compliance and ensuring that your tone is undemanding and empathetic, try asking your partner to work on changing one of those traits. Frame your request in an encouragingly positive way from the start.

Poor example: "We never go out. I want to have a weekly activity with you."

Good example: "I miss spending time with you away from the house. How would you feel about planning a weekly activity together?"

Day
6

Ending Couple Wars

Is this familiar?

You've been trying your best to communicate with your partner, and you truly want to come to some resolution, but every conversation just ends up in a fight.

Day 6 will help you understand how couples get into perpetual fighting cycles and ways to break out of them.

I see many couples who come to me saying, "I don't remember what we were even fighting about, or even how it started." One partner might start to question if it's a problem with them, rather than with the other person—or both. You may feel like a wall has come between you. And in some ways it may have, but it is not insurmountable.

Fights within a relationship begin with an attack—whether real or perceived—from one or both partners. This can trigger a defense and often end in retreat. It ultimately is not the context for the fight, but the hurt that the initial attack causes that damages your relationship. In a fight, your words and body language pack a punch that reflects your pain, anger, or fear, delivering the same painful experience upon your partner with force. In the midst of battle with your partner, you may be disinterested in pausing or listening, hitting hard below the belt. In couples therapy, I often hear a crosscurrent of careless words and strong implications that sweep the pair deeper into misunderstanding, leaving them exhausted and feeling more hopeless. Sometimes the argument is just a whirlpool that goes in circles and spins out of control, leaving each person feeling desperate and distant. Or even worse, both are trapped in iceberg silence, waiting for the other person to "break" loose.

Partners don't leave a relationship because they have different ideas about parenting, family time, or extended family; and not all fights destroy a relationship. Instead, relationships break apart when hurt, sadness, and fear have settled in as a resident. These lethal companions can show up every time an issue arises, whether it is overspending, disagreements about parenting, or how much time one is spending on social media. So powerful are these destructive companions that you don't hear your significant other's words; instead, you only feel the devastation of rejection and loss. Hurt comes in the form of shame, guilt, disappointment, and disillusionment; sadness follows betrayal and loss; and your greatest fear is that you are not loved, or even lovable. Such floods of emotions can be so reflexive you are rarely conscious of them, but you still feel the effect of them and react instinctively with an attack, defense, or withdrawal.

So, let's consider the true enemies of an intimate relationship, what I call the three weapons of couple wars:

- Attack Missiles
- Defense Armor
- Retreat/Cold War

When unhappy partners employ the weapons of attack, defense, and retreat, it causes the kind of hurt that sticks like a barb in the heart, evokes fear that the relationship is broken, and leads to razor-sharp anger. When unleashed, these painful emotions begin a reactive cycle leading to more attacks, defensiveness, and cold silence.

Let's examine how you attack, defend, or retreat in an unhealthy pattern of disagreement.

Attack Missiles

Attacks can be any combination of actions, gestures, and words that are loud or soft-spoken, manipulative, harshly critical, or plainly aggressive, and they can present in the form of both a frown and a smile. Attack bullets are used in multiple ways, such as to protest, criticize, complain, blame, demand, or cling.

The person on the receiving end of an attack missile counterattacks or pulls their armor on and moves to their defense.

Defense Armor

Retreat, distance, and cold logic are the protection you wear to cover your heart from injury and hide the worry that your significant other's love for you is ending. If you are taking a defensive position, your explanations of your feelings may sound like excuses, leaving the other person feeling that you don't listen and don't care. You may even occasionally leave your defensive position to deliver potshots or withdraw into silence. Defensiveness is primarily self-protection.

Retreat/Cold War

If partners begin to ignore each other's differences and deny each other's feelings, a cold war has already begun—even if this distance was originally created to avoid the hurt and stress caused by the previous attacks and defensiveness on either behalf.

A cold war can take the form of the following:

- Ultimate Retreat
- Silence and defeat
- Sadness
- Flight or freeze
- Feeling hopeless and insecure

Meanwhile, there are three patterns of every couple war, that we can understand as War #1, War #2, and War #3.

War #1 is a pattern of attack and defense: *When I push, you defend yourself and pull away.*

War #2 is a pattern of attack and counterattack. One-upmanship is needed to make the other one the "bad guy" and drive this pattern: *When I push, you push back harder.*

War #3 is a pattern of withdrawal from both parties: *When I pull away, you pull away. It's easier to stay away.*

Ending Couple Wars: A New Dynamic and Dialogue

Ending the cycle of fighting, defensiveness, or withdrawal requires that a couple pause long enough to understand and name the destructive dynamic that has developed within their relationship. Only in the rest period that the pause allows can two people rebuild their connection, attain a new understanding, and discuss how they can change. I describe the process of delay, rebuilding connection, and problem-solving as STOP + Listen + Show.

STOP + Listen + Show is a process built to allow a couple in crisis to regroup in a thoughtful and carefully paced way. STOP is our helpful acronym that refers to Stopping, Taking a breath, Observing and describing, and Planning.

By the time a couple gets to "P," they've exhibited healthy listening and productive showing. Let's understand this process in depth.

STOP (Stop, Take a breath, Observe and describe, Plan)

S.T.O.P.

When the negative spiral starts, visualize a red stop sign and say "STOP." Now is the time to create a shared awareness of your relationship's unhealthy cycle. Together, name this cycle. You can call it the Spin Cycle, or the Spiral Down, or the Black Hole. Now is the time to remember that your enemy is not your partner, but the cycle.

Take a breath.

When the negative spiral starts, slow down and work together to reduce your stress. Try to notice your physical distress such as an upset stomach or tightness in your throat, and remind yourself that your partner loves you and you are simply at the beginning of a cycle. Now slowly breathe. Let your partner know if you need a time-out and come to an agreement on when to return to the conversation.

Observe and describe.

Stay in the moment. Concentrate on keeping your body language and facial expressions calm and relaxed. Begin a new conversation with your partner for respectfully exploring what each of you say and do to sustain the harmful cycle.

Plan.

Reach for your partner and make a plan to solve the issue together. Your plan is more likely to succeed if you focus as much on the process of listening and showing as you do on the problem that needs to be resolved. Some form of touch may soothe and reinforce what you say.

Listen

Stay focused on what your partner says, and ask questions that show sincere interest. Avoid offering solutions without your partner's input.

Show

Be open and show your significant other that you care about what matters to them.

Let's consider several couples I have worked with to analyze the harmful dynamic they were experiencing and to understand how the attack/defense/retreat cycle played a role in their troubles. We'll notice how the couples' fights end when they say "STOP," then name the cycle, listen to each other, and explicitly show that they care for one another.

As we encounter each couple, we should remember that either party in a relationship can name their cycle. One partner might say, "Here we go, I complain, and you defend yourself. We're in the Complain–Defend cycle." One partner's observation about their cycle might help the other partner name the cycle themselves. For example, one partner might observe, "We are doing it again. You push and I push back," allowing the other to realize, "We're in a Push–Push cycle."

Another might formulate a different but equally well-founded cycle name. Both names will be informative as the couple works to understand and mitigate their cycle.

As we observe each session, we should also remember the importance of keeping communication clear between ourselves and our partner. We can do so by considering the following in any conversation:

- What we intend to say
- What we actually say
- What the other person hears
- What the other person thinks you meant

Each couple's example of their unique "war" should help us better understand how to regularly practice the STOP + Listen + Show method in healthy and productive ways.

(All the following names, scenarios, and dialogue have been revised for the purpose of this book.)

War One – Peggy and John: Attack/Defense
War One Template

- ☐ Attack: Complaint, criticism, or accusation expressed in words or body language
- ○ Defense: Dismissal, defensive response, freezing up, paralysis, and shutting down
- ☐ Attack: Persistent complaint or criticism with harsher rhetoric and body language
- ○ Defense: A shift of defense or a more stubborn silence

Background

Seven years into their relationship, Peggy threatened to leave John because he lacked emotional engagement and avoided showing tenderness and love. Hurt, he hid behind a calm exterior and distanced himself without voicing his worry that he was a failure, that there was nothing he could do, and that he had lost "everything."

When pressed, John said Peggy pushes until he reacts and pushes further until he overreacts. He believed he would never please Peggy, didn't have what it takes, and maybe wasn't meant to be married. John admitted he was confused.

Stop

John and Peggy name the dynamic between them as Push–Withdraw. They recognize that her complaints are a reaction to their loss of closeness.

> **Peggy:** I guess that my complaints are so upsetting that you leave the house to get away from them.
>
> **John:** I don't know what else to do. I am afraid to say the wrong thing and make you more upset. Then the whole day is ruined, and I feel even more helpless.

Take a Breath

The couple pauses to analyze their feelings and absorb what they discovered when they hit stop.

Observe (with Listening and Showing)

The couple observes and describes their fight as a reaction that does not actually represent how they feel about each other.

> **Peggy:** I know that I push hard. But it's because I don't get a response from you.
>
> **John:** So the spin cycle is: You push, I leave you upset and alone, you persist, trying even harder to get my attention, to make a connection, and I leave even more quickly.

John: I can see how this cycle has made us frustrated with each other and feel like there is no hope for our relationship.

Peggy: Being stuck in our negative feelings of disappointment, frustration, and hopelessness stops us from "seeing" and giving each other what we need.

Plan and Practice (with Listening and Showing)

The couple sees their old dialogue as a trap and begins to learn new words, body language, and actions. They say things that reinforce their connection and express reassurance.

John: You need me to be there with you physically and emotionally, and I need you to be understanding of my plans. That's not hard.

Peggy: When one of us notices that we are falling into the old pattern of "push and pull away," we will remember that the problem is our spin cycle and say, "let's STOP and redo."

John: Better yet, let's hug and hold before we redo.

War Two – Andrew and Susan: Attack/Counterattack.

War Two Template

- ☐ Attack: Hostile criticism, accusation, or nagging complaint expressed and reinforced by body language
- ○ Counterattack: Labeling the other person and proving them wrong maintains the cycle and reinforces hurt
- ☐ Attack: More criticism, escalation, and one-upmanship that ends when the fight is too stressful

Background

Andrew and Susan had been married for seventeen years, and Andrew said that he and Susan had periods of relative peace by avoiding each other, trying to be friendly, and hanging in there for the kids. Susan said that most of the time, she was numb or mad. Andrew added that Susan "goes on and on" until he eventually lashes out. He believed that the only way to deal with her was to fight back. But, beneath it all, they were both disappointed. They fought about parenting, her response to his family, his health choices, and overwork. He agreed that his family was overly demanding but attacked her family when she criticized him.

Stop
Andrew and Susan name the dynamic between them as Attack–Attack. They recognize that their attacks are a reaction to the loss of closeness.

> **Susan:** I get so hurt when your mother criticizes me. It's worse because you don't stand up for me. If I am tired, it doesn't take much for me to lose it.
>
> **Andrew:** I do stand up for you, but you don't seem to hear me. I am not as direct with my mother because I want to avoid a scene and protect the kids from the conflict.
>
> **Susan:** It hurts that you choose to criticize my family! It keeps the fight going. Then I start thinking that you are such a stranger and I wonder why I ended up with you. And if you think I am such a mess, why should I bother?
>
> **Andrew:** I brought up the fight with your sister just to get back at you. I accuse you so that you will back down. But we just end up hurting each other.

Take a Breath
The couple pauses to analyze their feelings and absorb what they discovered when they hit stop.

Observe (with Listening and Showing)
The couple observes and describes the fight as a reaction that does not represent how they actually feel about each other.

> **Susan:** So, the black hole is: I get hurt and complain, you lash out harder, I keep going with a bigger counterattack, and soon we are rehashing all our mistakes.

Andrew: I can see how this black hole has made us so hostile and cold to each other. Even when we aren't fighting, we are waiting for an attack.

Susan: When we aren't fighting, I think about the last thing you said. Being stuck in this coldness stops us from "seeing" and supporting each other.

Plan and Practice (with Listening and Showing)

The couple sees their old dialogue as a trap and begins to learn new words, body language, and actions to direct toward one another. They say things that reinforce their connection and express reassurance.

Andrew: You were right to speak up about my mother. I want you to come to me when you are hurt. It was wrong of me to bring up the incident with your sister.

Susan: Support from each other is all we need. That's not hard.

Andrew: When one of us notices that we are falling into the old pattern of "attack/counterattack," we will remember that the problem is the spin cycle and say, "let's STOP and redo."

Susan: Better yet, let's hug and hold before we redo.

War Three – Tim and Renée: Cold War/Retreat

War Three Template

- ☐ Pushing: Desperate attempts to engage
- ○ Avoidance: Disengagement in response to other reaching out
- ☐ Withdrawal: Disengagement as an answer to disengagement

Background

Tim and Renée had withdrawn from a romantic life. They had been married for seven years. Coldness, sadness, tension, living like friends, withdrawal, and indirect communication began to happen in waves at varying periods.

Renée said that she had tried unsuccessfully to get Tim to do things with her. Disappointed, she retreated, spending time with friends, hobbies, and parenting. Renée described herself as "numb" to Tim but less hurt. She remembered two years prior feeling that their marriage had "died." She stopped nagging and pushing, and now they were like the friends they were before attraction and dating. Tim didn't seem to care that Renée was detached, because he could now focus more on his career. Each led separate lives.

Stop

Tim and Renée named the dynamic between them as Push–Withdrawal, although Renée rarely tried to engage Tim any longer. They both agreed that silence and withdrawal were a reaction to the mutual loss of closeness.

> **Tim:** I am doing it again. Excusing myself by saying, "I am not meant to be in a relationship."
>
> **Renée:** I can't believe you noticed that! So, the spin cycle is: You exit the relationship by saying, "I am not meant to be in a relationship," I agree, and we go back to silence. The more you make "exit" moves, the more helpless and resigned I become.
>
> **Tim:** So, we're in an "Exit, Surrender" stage.

Take a Breath

The couple pause to analyze their feelings and absorb what they discovered when they hit stop.

Observe (with Listening and Showing)

The couple observes and describes their withdrawal as counterproductive to the health of their relationship.

> **Tim:** I want to be with you, and I know you are caring and good with people. My life would be empty without you.
>
> **Renée:** Tell me that sometimes and make plans with me.

Plan and Practice (with Listening and Showing)

The couple views their silence as a trap and begins to learn new words, body language, and actions to direct toward one another. They say things that reinforce their connection and express reassurance.

> **Tim:** If you can help me by pointing out my mistakes, I think I can stay and talk a bit.
>
> **Renée:** Being understanding and engaging with each other is all we need. That's not hard.

Dealing with the By-Products of Couple Wars: Stress and Negativity

Fighting reliably remains an ineffective ploy to regain a safe emotional connection. In a fight, we experience various levels of stress that stop us from being rational, making logical decisions, and having compassion. It is nearly impossible to listen, ask questions, and see our partner's perspective in a time of strain. We would always rather, if we could, recognize the power struggle and egos at play and address our issues cooperatively instead of throwing barbs. All of us would prefer to have the clarity of mind to call a time-out, relax, and understand that a disagreement does not mean we have lost control or that our love relationship is slipping away.

Even more dangerous to our relationships are the intense emotions that become hardwired as a record of a negative event. Such emotions will return when any threat to the relationship resurfaces. In these moments we may respond by "going numb," saying, "I don't know, it doesn't matter, or I don't care," further distancing us from achieving the goal of reconnection.

We must remember that we would never have settled in with our partners if our early dating and coupling encounters weren't warm, comforting, and connecting. However, here you find yourself, wondering why you don't get along. You have both individually changed so much, perhaps, that you've forgotten how to support, admire, and nurture each other as you once did! Even so, until you remove the armor and lower the guns, no real talk can happen. Worse, if you don't, you are decidedly ending the relationship, setting aside any opportunity to grow and flourish both as individuals and as a couple.

Following are some ways to help alleviate the stress and negativity that come from fighting.

Pause and Reflect

We have been told not to go to bed angry, to deal with issues right away so they don't fester—both ideal suggestions for couples . . . if only we could always remain calm, logical, rational, and caring in the middle of a disagreement! The truth is, in the middle of an argument, whether it be about doing more housework or not spending enough time together, a part of your brain called the amygdala activates—that little almond-shaped gland in our temporal lobes that is triggered if we were to see, say, a black bear racing toward us. We then experience the release of adrenalin, cortisol, epinephrine, and norepinephrine, leaving our heart beating faster, blood pressure spiking, and chest tightening, making us respond more "loudly" to our situation and less aware of the consequences of our behavior.[1] Ultimately, the real culprit behind our poor choice of words and irrational decisions in a fight is the reduced blood flow to our prefrontal cortex, the place where our best decisions are made.

So we must practice becoming more and more aware when we're under the spell of our amygdala and force ourselves to pause. But we are not pausing in order to find a space to disappear, or to ask for a friend's advice, and definitely not to take more time to simmer and construct new painful scenarios. We are pausing to calm ourselves and regulate our emotions through simple, slow, deep breaths. Of course, there are other ways to train down your emotions, but the breath is available and calms you every time. Emotional regulation, in fact, has been found to predict marriage satisfaction. In a thirteen-year study of long-term married couples published in 2014, couples were reported as being more capable of productively communicating after mutually achieving emotional regulation.[2]

Practice Vulnerability

When Tim said to Renée, "I am doing it again," he took ownership of being human, fallible and in need of help. He accepted the possibility of criticism and demonstrated real strength and courage by the admission of his "failure." In doing so, he found himself able to say, "Here I am—my relationship struggles, my worst fears, my not-always-enough love. Be good to me." In response, Renée told him, "I see you. You don't need to change who you are. You are safe with me." Vulnerability doesn't guarantee relationship success. Nothing can. But without the openness, trust-building, closeness, and sense of belonging that vulnerability offers, a relationship is lifeless and disconnected.

Using what you have learned about the three styles of couple wars, work on the table below with your partner. The table gives you and your partner an opportunity to pinpoint the type of war you're currently in and to create a name for the unhealthy behavior cycle that is perpetuating this war. The table also gives you space to take note of unhealthy ways each of you begin dialogues, as well as space to brainstorm healthy alternatives. As these are dialogue "starters," you will be thinking specifically of ways each of your statements begin. You can use the couples' conversations above for reference on unhealthy versus healthy ways to engage in dialogue.

Type of War We're In	Name for Our Cycle
Example: Attack–Attack	Example: Push–Push Harder
Old Dialogue Starters **(When We Should STOP)**	**New Dialogue Starters** **(Ways to Listen and Show)**
Examples: "I hate it when you . . . " "You always forget to . . . "	Examples: "It hurts me when you forget to . . . " "Can we find a way to . . . ?"

Type of War We're In	Name for Our Cycle
Old Dialogue Starters (When We Should STOP)	New Dialogue Starters (Ways to Listen and Show)

Reflection | Day 6: Ending Couple Wars

Points to Remember

It is not what you are fighting about but the hurt of the attack that breaks the relationship. Your partner is not the enemy. The adversary is the negative spin cycle and downward spiral that takes you into the black hole of hurt.

Questions to Consider

Could you solve problems more efficiently if you stated disagreements calmly? If there were no threat of criticism (attack), defense, or withdrawal, would you speak up more honestly? If your partner routinely thanked you for speaking up, would you be open and vulnerable?

Action Plan

Identify how you fight with you partner by filling in the blanks:

> **Partner A:** When you _____, I don't feel connected and I cope by _____, hoping you will _____. The more this happens, the more I begin to believe that _____. When I look at this pattern, it is clear that I am on the attack, defense, or have withdrawn.
> **Partner B:** Thank you for _____.

Example:

> **Partner A:** I reneged on my promise to do the renovations because you were so angry when I raised concerns about the cost.
> **Partner B:** Thanks for being honest with me. I remember lashing out because I was afraid that you would let me down and not do the renovations. I guess I wasn't listening. Tell me about your concerns. I am listening to you now.
> *Notice: Partner A uses an "I" statement. They don't attack. Partner B does not make excuses for their actions (defense). Partner B may or may not agree with Partner A, but they allow Partner A to have their reasons.*

Intentional Communication Strategies

Is this familiar?

You think you're telling your partner one thing, but they're hearing another. You think you're giving your partner one signal, but they're taking an entirely different message from it than you intended—and it just keeps stretching the distance between the two of you.

Day 7 will give you tips and tools for enhancing the romantic aspect of your relationship with effective, dynamic communication strategies.

The word "romance" conjures up images of date nights, love notes, candlelight, compliments, sexting, impromptu flowers, prepared bedsheets, and wild nights of playtime. However, couples often forget these aspects as they navigate real life, which is full of obligations and distractions. I've heard both men and women express sentiments like, "I rush home for a date night but am too tired to enjoy it," or "When he gets me flowers it makes me wonder what he wants." These comments highlight the need for romance to be more than superficial gestures. It is really a need for commitment rooted in meaningful connection and attachment—both promoted by intentional communication.

The communication I encourage uses words, eyes, ears, and, essentially, whole bodies. Such communication conveys to each partner that they are special, valued, and secure. When your partner experiences you in this way, they reciprocate with tenderness and openness. Intentional whole-body communication emphasizes the power of listening, making an effort to avoid mixed messages, and employing two-step dialogue that nurtures romance.

While you may desire certainty that romance will endure and your partner will remain attentive and responsive, such guarantees don't exist. Instead, security comes from effective communication and the resulting connection.

You may claim to be a good communicator because you speak up without hesitation, talk a lot, or have a good vocabulary. You trust the feedback of work colleagues, family members, or friends who commend your presentation. However, a couple's relationship is different from family, friendship, professional, or casual relationships in that it demands a distinct level of engagement. Nothing but the highest level of support, honesty, tenderness, acceptance, and respect will satisfy the demands of committed love. You provide this only with intentional communication designed to foster connection.

I confess that I am as easily caught up in the age of information and distraction as anyone else. I have at times become so immersed in my own progress that I have neglected to slow down and experience the exchange of listening, restating, and fully understanding. But the threat of joining the ranks of the lonely, disconnected, and panic-stricken has forced me into a more authentic way of being. I am a true believer in relationships being based on thoughtful and conscious communication.

We can follow these four strategies to enhance our communication and connection with our partners:

- Use body language
- Listen mindfully
- Avoid mixed messages
- Dialogue effectively

Body Language: Use Your Body as the Amplifier It Is

Ever wonder why you seem to push your partner away when you try so hard to be understood? Is it you? Is it them? Consider that the culprit may be your posture, facial expressions, gestures, or voice.

Maybe you see yourself in John and Susan. Both intelligent and well-intentioned, in one of our early sessions, they settled into armchairs across from each other, ignoring the love seat—understandable behavior when you are not getting along. However, it was the two contracted lines between John's brows that hinted at his contempt, not his words: "I want to stay together." He folded his arms and clenched his jaw without making an effort to relax and soften his eye contact.

Susan reacted with sarcasm, anger, and criticism. They avoided eye contact, and neither party acknowledged John's verbalized desire.

Think about your body as a billboard with bold graphics broadcasting an advertisement for what you are thinking and feeling. You "soften" or "harden" the message with smiles and open-body posture or scowls and frowns. Your body language must demonstrate your resolve and desire to improve and collaborate with your significant other or they won't believe your words. If you are ever in John's position, consider the person sitting across the room and your stated goal to repair your relationship. Connect to and acknowledge your feelings and adjust your body language to reflect an accurate message with the following suggestions.

Focus on visualization and relaxation. Your face and body reflect your stress. Take a few minutes to decompress by visualizing a calm and relaxing scene.

Present yourself as a calm and thoughtful person. In all but the most extreme circumstances, remaining calm in any kind of conflict will de-escalate the dialogue and improve your ability to make good decisions—even if you don't feel that way in the moment.

Sustain calmness by "softening" yourself, projecting warmth and care into your eyes, voice, tone, touch, and bodily movements. This softening helps keep the conversation upbeat and improves your connection.

Listen Mindfully: Ensure the Person Special to You Feels Heard

"Listening is a magnetic and strange thing, a creative force" psychiatrist Karl A. Menninger is attributed to having once observed. "The friends who listen to us are the ones we move toward. When we are listened to, it creates us, makes us unfold and expand." In other words, listening may be the shortest path to someone's heart. So, retrain yourself to listen actively with a sincere desire to know and understand your partner and their point of view. This kind of mindful listening focuses only on what your significant other says and prevents distraction. Mindful listening is the opposite of selective listening where the person waits for a turn to speak and neglects to give feedback. To reinforce mindful listening, notice when you have tuned out and are missing valuable content, then make an effort to renew your focus, utilizing the strategy of placing yourself in the other person's shoes.

Listening tells the person you are tracking with them and that they matter. Strive to practice these behaviors in engaged listening:

- Listen for words and meaning.
- Reserve judgment and opinion.
- Seek only to understand.
- Ask questions to enhance understanding, and occasionally summarize, to be precise.
- Keep your body language friendly and open.
- Look into your significant other's eyes when they are speaking.

Stephen R. Covey, author of *The 7 Habits of Highly Effective People: Powerful Lessons in Personal Change*, says, "Most people do not listen with the intent to understand; they listen with the intent to reply."[1] Whatever the content of your reply, beware of being a "fixer" or "know-it-all" who can't resist the urge to select the faults of an argument or person and correct them. Beware of falling into the trap of the egoic need to be the one who is "always right."

Mindful or deep listening is a sure way to stimulate your personal growth, prevent quick, defensive responses, and strengthen a connection. It tells the person on the receiving end that they are valuable. It is a way of showing love and is the soul of healthy communication.

Avoid Mixed Messages: Communicate to Build Trust and Avoid Confusion

When your body language, behavior, and words send a message that contradict what you're actually feeling, your partner will end up being confused and not knowing what to trust.

The following example demonstrates that even well-meaning couples can be dishonest and inconsistent in their messaging to one another.

Art and Jenny enjoyed relaxing in bed on Saturday mornings. After a week of commuting and going in different directions, they rested and felt like themselves again. One day Art casually mentioned that his boss had invited him to join a golf foursome on Saturday mornings. Just for the summer.

Jenny could feel the loss of their Saturday mornings as if it were a physical blow—but she immediately discounted her loss and rationalized, "Art works so hard, he deserves some time to relax."

As the summer advanced, Jenny's hurt feelings surfaced in many ways. She was irritable on weekends and made plans with friends when John was expecting to spend time with her. Yet whenever he asked if she was upset, she always simply said, "No."

I have heard individuals say there's nothing wrong in a session with a partner, but alone, they vent anger, frustrations, and resentments about that very person.

In our relationships we need to continually ask each other questions, agree to be open about our distresses and needs, and resolve the issues between us before they become a source of resentment. Like a bubbling volcano, disappointments worsen, compound, and eventually explode.

Dialogue Effectively: Two-Step Your Conversation with Restatement and Validation

Dialogue is like a dance. Just as you wouldn't think of waltzing to the other side of the room and leaving your partner standing, you shouldn't hijack the conversation. Instead, pay attention to your partner's body language, make room for them to enter the conversation, and focus on the issue at hand. Let's consider some suggestions to keep the two-way conversation flowing:

Limit yourself to one or two statements, and don't "run away" with the topic.

Avoid "You" as the opener to express your frustrations and hurt. Instead, use "I" statements. "I" signals responsibility while "You" sends a message of accusation (regardless of whether you mean to or not). Your goal is to send clear signals that help you stay connected in or out of a fight.

The steps to good dialogue are listening, restating, validation, and empathy, and using them is like learning a new language. At first, it seems awkward and impossible to remember, but if you persist, each step slows the conversation down so that you can understand and digest what the other person is saying, while also giving you the space to provide feedback.

1. Listening is the active and mindful process that we discussed earlier.
2. Restating is how you know you have heard, understood, or even felt your significant other's emotion. It is a response, not an agreement, and your partner should feel relieved, relaxed, and understood. Restatement reduces the likelihood of defensiveness that brings the conversation to an end, stymies connection, or reduces the possibility of problem-solving.
3. Validation is how you tell your significant other that their thoughts and feelings are acceptable.
4. Empathy is how you identify with your partner.

In the following example of a typical fight between John and Susan, I have shown how to put into practice the steps to good dialogue.

Attack

John: You seemed delighted to see the Jones family. (Sarcasm followed by a brief silence.) You spent so much time complimenting Donny on his promotion and barely spoke to me all evening. (Hurt and increased volume of voice.) I am sure everyone heard you, and I felt like a loser. (Use of the accusatory "You.")

Defensive Response

Susan: I hadn't seen the Joneses in a long time. I was genuinely glad to see them. The man just got a promotion. What did you want me to do?

Here is an alternative model for dialogue that would help John and Susan resolve their differences and modify future behavior.

John: I am upset that you were so happy to see the Jones family, how much you complimented Donny on his promotion, and that you barely spoke to me all evening.

Keeping an even, conversational tone and being succinct helps John manage his hurt and anger and allows Susan to respond thoughtfully instead of reactively.

Restatement

Susan: I get it. You're upset that I was "over the top" with the Jones family, complimented Donny, and didn't notice you very much. Is that what you are saying?

Susan's restatement is not an admission of guilt or fault. Instead, the purpose is to clarify and understand.

John: I have nothing against Donny. I only felt like I didn't exist.

John responds with a goal of preventing misunderstanding and clarifying his feelings.

Validation

Susan: I can see how you would feel that way. I was angry at you and didn't care if I made you mad.

The purpose of validation is to highlight the other person's words or genuine qualities and not pacify with platitudes. Therefore, the movement toward peace is built from an honest place.

Empathy: The Key to Healing

Susan: Seeing that you felt so unimportant, are you still hurt and upset with me?

What does it take for a couple to begin responding to each other with restatement and validation when differences or sensitive issues arise? How can they ensure that they are not looking for a formula for winning versus a recipe for a "win-win" solution?

A person who listens consciously and is genuinely interested in the person speaking leaves that person feeling respected, valued, and with a sense of confidence and competence. The following is the story of my friend Prim, whose personality blossomed through a relationship with a great communicator. Prim's experience illustrates the person we can be in our partner's life.

About twelve years ago, Prim, an HR manager in a corporate setting, described a new colleague with the comment, "Bayo is the best communicator I have ever met and perhaps the wisest human being." I dismissed my friend's comments as idle chatter but noticed a change in her personality as she befriended Bayo. I felt his effect on her personality as Prim became more present and genuinely interested in others and the world around her. She had a newfound confidence and self-concept that opened new doors and freedoms for her. When I met Bayo, it was clear that his gift was listening and understanding the people around him. As an avid reader and writer who had lived among many cultures, he still chose to listen generously and curiously to those around him in preference to sharing his own wisdom and experiences. Bayo listened with his whole body inclined and his eyes focused on his subject. The questions he asked left you in no doubt that he had heard your words and placed himself in your shoes.

The quality of Bayo's friendship began an unfolding in Prim's life that prompted her to challenge and end a one-sided but long-standing love relationship. In the oasis of his listening presence, she sparkled and shed the belief that she was unattractive and unlovable. Prim ventured into online dating with the balanced and relaxed attitude of one who had already found a significant other in themselves.

> *"Communication is a learnable skill. It's something that we can actually train ourselves in—which means that it takes time, it takes effort, and that we need to have a method. We can't just think about it and get better at communication. We actually need to do exercises to learn and relearn these habits."*
> —Oren Jay Sofer

Reflection | Day 7:
Intentional Communication Strategies

Points to Remember
Connection, intimacy, and romance are enhanced by learning and practicing a different approach to communication.

Questions to Consider
Ask your significant other which of the following is most needed to build a stronger connection: Conscious body language? Mindful listening? Clear messaging? Or constructive dialogue?

Action Plan
In the next four weeks, practice each of the four dialogue skills until they become a familiar language:
- Listening (week one)
- Restating (week two)
- Validating (week three)
- Empathy (week four)

Day
8

Moving from I to We

Is this familiar?

You believe that cooperation and collaboration are intuitive and, disappointed in your partner's behavior, you say to yourself, "They think only about themselves. It's like I don't even exist."

Day 8 gives you the tools to move from living as a single unit to a mutual relationship.

What does it look like when partners act like singles? One carries the load of the housework and childcare. Every suggestion you make is met with protests. The TV blares loudly while you try to read . . . You wonder if your partner loves you.

A lasting relationship needs more than common interests and physical chemistry, more than empty words and puny effort. It begs for unity and togetherness that converts a morning of housecleaning from a sense of labor into accomplishment. A relationship lasts when different interests can be enjoyed together, and complex situations can be transformed into bonding experiences. Such relationships put a premium on time together, partner focus, and selflessness, all in order to build pillars of agreement and honor interdependence. Enjoyed in combination, couples may build deep friendship and a sense of community that keeps the relationship intact and thriving.

Why It Is Important to Be Part of a Team

There are some couples who glide into cohabitation without a glitch. They pour their talents into the tasks of the home, collaborate on projects, and give without compromising their individuality. These couples have a healthy compassion for each other, goals that are aligned, and a willingness to communicate their needs in an open and trusting manner. This is not always the case, and many couples struggle with partnership; one or both, in fact, may continue to live as if they were single. There are also many more who have been taught to believe that leaning on others is a weakness and that helping others along the way somehow creates scarcity in their life. These beliefs are counterproductive to a couple's community building.

I had lunch with my friend Andrew a while ago, excited to hear about his climb to the summit of Machu Picchu and his experiences along the way. Listening intently and expecting to *ooh* and *aah* my way through, I was moved as he described the help he had from coaches and trainers through his early days of overtraining and buying the wrong gear. "I would never have made it," he said, "without the advice of seasoned climbers who told me what clothes to take and what snacks were best."

After months of training, a year of research and preparation, Andrew realized a lifelong dream. When I asked him what was most memorable of his experience, he said, "Of course, the summit, but I will never forget our little group. We sang, we laughed, we listened and helped each other out every day." He said his memory of the misty mornings, the many Incan ruins, and the breathtaking views might be forgotten someday, but the stories told, and the meals shared would always be etched in his mind. He described an African American woman from Buffalo who saved from her overtime pay to bond with her nineteen-year-old before he went to college, girlfriends celebrating a milestone birthday, and a fitness guru and his followers.

Stories like this touch us because we know deep down that a life without caring is shallow and the connection we crave comes only from people. But we have also been told to be independent, and to avoid dependence and codependence, and therefore we may be confused about what is healthy. We are wary about being too needy. But interdependence is always the healthy option. It is necessary for us to maintain our connection with one another and ward off the ever-growing epidemic of loneliness—mostly found, as it turns out, in first-world countries.

Interdependence in Grief and Loss

Loneliness has long been a serious problem in North America, and the COVID pandemic had made it worse for many. A report based on an online survey of 950 Americans in October 2020 determined that "36% of all Americans—including 61% of young adults and 51% of mothers with young children—feel 'serious loneliness.' " One of the report's key recommendations was "to restore our commitment to each other and the common good."[1]

One contributing factor to loneliness may be the decline in marriages worldwide. In the United States, for example, less than half of all adults are married compared to 72% in 1960,[2] and those who are married are doing so later than in years past.[3] Some writers have speculated that the reason for this statistical decline is that people are cohabiting without formal marriage, avoiding the struggle of divorce, and giving themselves more freedom and choice. As the nuclear family is replaced, it is clear that we must rethink how we will bond and be accountable and responsible to each other.

About four years ago, my South Asian friend Nesta traveled to California from Toronto to grieve the passing of her uncle with her relatives. She set aside her family responsibilities (a big deal for her), closed the flower shop she had opened just one month prior, and made the trip she couldn't afford. She returned a week later, visibly refreshed, and re-immersed herself in her business. When I asked, she described seven days when all the women sat in a circle on the floor or chairs and shared their photos and stories of "Uncle Hata." They took turns cooking for each other, crying, and sipping sweet tea. Music played in the background or was forgotten, sometimes they lit candles and sometimes they didn't. People came and left as they needed, but everyone was embraced and welcome. "It's easy to move on when you have grieved with your friends and relatives," she said. Psychotherapist Francis Weller echoes the same sentiment in his book *The Wild Edge of Sorrow: Rituals of Renewal and the Sacred Work of Grief.* "What I have discovered in grief rituals over many years is that we feel relief when we finally are able to acknowledge our pain with one another."[4]

We can't avoid sickness, loss, and disappointment, nor can we predict betrayal and heartbreak. Those are the times when the only thing that helps is a shoulder to cry on, someone to listen and reassure us that tomorrow is another day. When we have graduated, gotten a promotion, bought a first home, or heard that we are to become grandparents, we want the people we love to beam their delight. We need them to say, "Good job, I'm so proud of you," or boost our confidence with, "You'll be great at it!" The people that we need most of all are our significant others.

In our relationships we must avoid the one-sidedness of codependence, dependence, and even independence, rather working toward an interdependence that ensures each partner is empowered to care for one another practically and emotionally.

Steps to Building a Team

Do you remember the early days of dating when you drove past the other person's house hoping there was time for a nightcap? You talked into the wee hours and discovered how much you had in common. They helped you with crafts, and you contributed to their own projects; you devoted time to hanging out and having long discussions, all the while building a strong connection that imbued your relationship with a sense of certainty and commitment to your love.

After the extreme togetherness of a new romance, it is natural that you and your partner gradually return to individual interests, goals, responsibilities, and obligations. Your separate lives can become a problem, however, if they end up occupying so much time that you become strangers to one another.

Countless couples spend too much time away from their spouse and later find themselves facing a stranger but still hoping for a relationship. They have perhaps discovered that they never built the synergy and tenderness critical to maintaining a lasting connection.

I witnessed this kind of poorly laid foundation with a couple who came to me after the husband retired; both agreed that they got along better before he retired. In this case, Roger had spent his twenty-five-year career traveling and indulging his passion for golf while Margie enjoyed home decorating and nurturing her friendships. They couldn't understand why the dream of retirement paled in the face of daily frustrations, fights, and general unhappiness with each other.

Some couples are proud of how well they coordinate their lives, dividing and conquering the "to-do list" and kid's activities. One takes the highway, and the other does the local running around. Such a couple ends up living in a sort of "business relationship" tied together by parallel lives, and the continual time apart leads to a sense of distance between partners. This is how one can end up with the feeling that they're married to a stranger.

To some extent, all couples are at risk of experiencing the following cascade of events:

- Busyness, distraction, fatigue → Little energy remaining for anything but critical priorities
- Your significant other is not a priority → You neglect and, in turn, feel neglected
- Your connection fails → Disconnection prompts disagreements, contempt, fights, and withdrawal
- Hurt and loss → More withdrawal
- Loneliness → Filling your life with others or new interests

Couples don't expect this to happen, and partners may become surprised at the shift in the other or in themselves.

To avoid the pitfalls of being a stranger to our significant others, we must cultivate a model of interdependence and find the right balance. Once interdependence is established, the next steps are to focus on finding agreement and making it a priority to focus on our partners.

Interdependence

Maybe you grew up in a family where independence was highly valued and reinforced or learned that depending on others is scary and unpredictable. You worry that releasing autonomy means becoming dependent or codependent. Interdependence is neither dependence nor independence. It is a balance of yourself and your significant other within the relationship, recognizing that both partners are working to be present and meet each other's physical and emotional needs in appropriate and meaningful ways. Partners need to know they are not alone in the relationship and can find support from each other.

When a couple decides to live interdependently—forming a "we-ship"—they ask:

- Are we making important decisions together?
- Do we share the same vision? Are we accommodating each other's personal vision?
- Is there equity and agreement in the way we use time, money, and skills?
- Are we equally involved in activities?
- Do we need to change our expectations regarding household and other tasks?
- Are we offering emotional support and care?

No longer seeing each other as solitary beings, the couple embraces healthy sacrifice and selflessness by beginning to work together to infuse their relationship with mutual empowerment, nurture, and the ease that comes with joy.

Consider creating a relationship vision that helps you practice interdependence and shifts your thinking from I to We. Collaborate on everyday topics such as money, sex, work, parenting, and housework.

Remember that interdependence leaves you space to be yourself, but also allows you to be vulnerable, does not compromise boundaries, and involves consistent check-ins that keep you bonded and attached.

Agreement

In the early days of dating, couples notice the many things they have in common—such as similar tastes in art and similar past experiences—and they find harmony among many of their values and beliefs. This early, strong bonding promotes mutual responsiveness that sustains the relationship with lightness and joy.

The disappointment comes later when too many conversations result in one person playing the "devil's advocate" as they feel more and more comfortable being opinionated and even argumentative with the other. I am not suggesting that you don't cultivate your own separate opinions and have lively debates, but I hope that you also continue to recognize the ways in which you agree with your partner, what you share in personalities, and the opportunities before you for working together in harmony.

How do couples emphasize shared values and agreement? They honor a shared culture. This culture may be expressed in the meals they enjoy together, in anniversaries and birthdays, and even in simple rituals of everyday togetherness, like snuggling together on the couch—a culture reserved just for them.

Partner Focus

Before settling in together with your partner, your chief focus was satisfying your own needs. Things like what you wanted to do in your spare time, how you entertained yourself, where and what you ate, and the friends you wanted to spend time with occupied your thoughts and decision-making.

Even before adulthood, a parent may have placed an excess of attention on your needs. After decades of focus on you, there is a risk that you move into a relationship expecting to maintain what feels like the natural order. Imagine your significant other having a similar expectation, and after a few months or years, you are both disappointed, saying to yourselves, "They think only about themselves." There is no better time than at this juncture for each partner to decidedly shift their focus onto the other and begin thinking of themselves as a team.

After years of research into why couples repeatedly say, "He/she doesn't love me," relationship expert Dr. Gary Chapman discovered that there are five distinct ways to express and receive love, each act of love representing something we need from our partners but is often missing in whole or in part. In his book *The Five Love Languages*, Chapman lays out each love language and gives advice on how to effectively shift your partner focus in order to "reach" them and elicit healthy responses from them.[5]

Here are Chapman's five expressions of love:

Words of Affirmation. From cradle to grave we want the people who care for us to say that we are doing well, that they admire and are proud of us. Let's ensure our compliments, acknowledgements, and encouragement are generous, sincere, and unsolicited.

Quality Time. Do more together and make memories. One couple I know, Laura and Anton, married at age eighteen and have been together for twenty-five years. I happened to be in a group discussion about vacation time recently and Laura was specific about being unavailable on the weekends when her spouse was not at work. She was graceful in enduring the gentle teasing of her friends and pointed out that she misses Anton when they have been apart too long. This couple shares hobbies and interests and openly prioritize their anniversaries, getaways, and special celebrations.

Receiving Gifts. This can be misunderstood as materialism, but Dr. Chapman is clear in his explanation that gift-giving as a means to show your significant other that they are supported and loved is an act that says, "I was thinking about you when I saw this. You're always on my mind."

Acts of Service. In relationship terms, these acts are not just things your significant other would like, but they are especially thoughtful gestures that I call "heartwarming actions." My husband fills the car with gas, clears the snow in the winter, and changes the winter tires at the end of the season—unasked and unannounced. He goes to the grocery store, picks up dry cleaning and organizes the garage without a list, fanfare, or accolades. These are the small things I don't enjoy doing but still don't take for granted, since they are all so important. My husband may never go on a hike with me, join me in yoga, or spend hours talking about certain topics I myself never tire of—but his acts of service prompt me to learn more about his needs and ensure they are met.

Physical Touch. Skin contact releases hormones associated with pleasure and bonding, and I believe physical touch *absolutely needs* to be on every couple's list as a want, if not a love language. Through touch the body secretes serotonin, dopamine, and oxytocin, leaving you feeling good. If love is not a natural language for you, experiment with cuddling, kissing, sitting on the other's lap, and, my favorite, just holding. With each gesture, concentrate on breathing, relaxing the body, and noticing your responses.

Each expression of love is important. Don't assume that your partner wants words of affirmation because you do. Ask them and notice their response when you express one language or another. Learning your partner's and your own primary love language will help create a stronger bond in your relationship.

Selflessness

In a discussion with Oprah about true love, wisdom teacher and mystic Father Richard Rohr explained that true love is "the death of the false self," and to fall in love is to risk changing yourself for the other person. "The inability to selflessly give yourself over to another person," he adds, "is the ultimate relationship downfall. No matter how much you may try to ignore it, there's no escaping its fate. If you don't give your friend, your partner, the power to change you, I don't think you love them. And your unconscious knows that. Your soul knows that."[6]

Carry Your Share

Have you said, "I have to do it all," in response to the overwhelming feeling that comes from being in a relationship where you can't count on your partner to do their share?

When a couple enters a union of two or a family of more, and one continues to live as a single person, the relationship becomes strained and unbalanced. One person is doing too much, the other too little, and discontentment soon sets in.

As a relationship therapist, I have encountered many situations in which even married partners still insist on living like bachelors and bachelorettes, primarily doing things that serve themselves and not the other.

In one scenario, a husband tried to congratulate his wife for breaking gender barriers when he complimented her on being "just as capable as men," doing things such as taking the garbage out and mowing the lawn. It was only then, however, that his wife revealed, "And everything *else* too!"

In another scenario, a husband complained that he just couldn't count on his wife to participate in time set aside for togetherness. He explained that they would make a plan together, but his wife would often suddenly cancel to hang out with her friends instead. She even agreed with him in our session.

Often, a partner has grown so acclimated to serving themselves before serving their relationship, never fully shifting from a "bachelor/bachelorette" mindset to a partner mindset, that they simply cannot see the imbalance they are creating until the other feels empowered to speak up.

Alone Time Is Okay

Everyone benefits from some time alone to varying degrees. For this reason, it is important that you communicate your alone-time needs to your partner.

If you indulge in an excess of solitude, however, you run the risk of your partner beginning to feel alone and disconnected from you, and you may find you're actually living in single cells instead of a unit of two.

We should remember that we do not have to change our own personalities to maintain our bond with our partner—but we do need to participate in couple or family activities, problem-solve as a team, and provide loving interactions that tell the other person they are not alone in the relationship, and that you want to pull your weight in a "we-ship."

Sharing a Team Vision

Successful relationships are not only based on partners acting conscientiously toward one another, but in *visualizing* their relationship together in a spirit of unity. One activity that couples can use as a tool to form a shared vision is the "relationship vision" exercise, conceived by couples therapist and author Harville Hendrix and laid out in his book *Getting the Love You Want: A Guide for Couples.* The "relationship vision" exercise provides a framework for couples to bring their mutual goals and desires into focus.[7] The following are simplified directions for the exercise, performed by each partner individually:

1. On separate sheets of paper, describe what you feel is a satisfying love relationship. You should include cherished qualities your relationship already has, as well as qualities your relationship does not currently have but you wish did. Statements should begin with "We" and kept concise and positive in tone (that is, "We come to peaceful resolutions," rather than, "We don't get into arguments").

2. Share your statements with your partner, underlining any items that you have in common, while, for the moment, ignoring items that are not shared. Add sentences to your own list for items your partner thought of and you hadn't, but with which you agree.

3. Rate the importance of each item using a range of 1 through 10, 1 indicating least importance, 10 indicating extremely important.

4. Circle the two items that are most important to you.

5. Put a check beside the items you feel will be the most difficult to achieve.

6. Work together to design a mutual relationship vision using the example below.[8] Hold on to your vision, perhaps displaying it in a place you both will regularly see, and focus on remembering your partner's priorities. Dedicate a page in a relationship journal to

your present vision, updating as needed (a couple's relationship journal can help each member stay on track in following through on decisions and remembering insights).

Partner A	Our Relationship Vision	Partner B
10	We are sexually faithful.	10
6	We are financially secure.	8
8	We have fun together.	7
6	We support each other's career goals.	6
4	We have a healthy lifestyle.	8
5	We have a clutter-free home.	7

Reflection | Day 8: Moving from I to We

Points to Remember
Being a team strengthens the emotional bond and guards against selfishness, loneliness, and competition.

Questions to Consider
Are you contributing time and effort to your relationship? Are you truly engaged with your partner? Ask your partner if, at any time, in any area, they feel overworked or taken for granted.

Action Plan
Complete the relationship vision exercise and have weekly check-ins with your partner to measure your relationship satisfaction.

Dealing with Criticism from Your Partner

Is this familiar?

You feel like everything from your partner is a criticism or correction. You silently say to yourself, "I can't do anything right. They know everything."

I have met many people who have suffered from being with such a partner. Day 9 provides tips on how to nip it in the bud.

In 1986, psychologists and researchers John Gottman and Robert Levenson built what became known as the "Love Lab."[1] It was an apartment where they observed more than three thousand couples, evaluating facial expressions, heart rate, blood pressure, skin conductivity, and conversations. They found that criticism opens the door to other negative states that lead to separation and divorce. Furthermore, if unchecked, it can lead to defensiveness, contempt, and stonewalling, and may result in a permanent break, causing a partner to forget what they saw in the other in the first place. Essentially, criticism makes your significant other feel unworthy, focuses unfairly on their flaws, and de-emphasizes their positive traits.

Excessive criticism from a partner may indeed dissipate those initial starry-eyed feelings of romance and connection. But there are ways to dismantle the walls that criticism builds up over time—the key is to first distinguish the kinds of criticism we may receive from our partners.

Recognize Criticism

Not all criticism is blatant and overt, but can rather be disguised in the form of subtle jabs, offhanded unfavorable comparisons, or even expressed as only "meant to be constructive." Overt or subtle, no form of criticism is helpful to the long-term health of any relationship.

We may not always recognize we're being criticized in the moment, but the body has a boundary against "assault" by criticism, so don't ignore it! It could feel like a punch in your gut or a pain in your heart. When communicating with your partner, pay attention to negative physical responses occurring within you, as well as your emotional reaction, including thoughts that seem to scream "No!"—and speak up. From there, try to recognize the specific ways that criticism from your partner may show its face. It could be in their blaming, complaining, mocking, or use of "you" statements that are followed by a negative judgment; it could be in their asking you to be and do something you don't want to. It could even come in the form of their body language as they speak.

The purpose of recognizing criticism is not to counterattack or defend but to address the issues generating the criticism itself. "Getting back" at your loved one or proving them wrong will not make them less critical. The goal is to build a mutual understanding and help your partner reform their mode of expressing discontent or frustration in a healthy way.

All couples experience disappointment in each other from time to time. After all, you grew up in different homes, with your own brand of DNA, marching to a drum only you hear. As we've discussed, though, your differences are healthy, nourishing your relationship and making it more dynamic. Differences between partners only become a problem when one or the other interprets them as an imposition—or even an attack—on them.

Jonah and Carol's story is an example of a couple caught in a cycle of criticism. The couple began counseling after several failed attempts to resolve their differences. After ten minutes into the meeting, she detailed his faults and, when he had enough, Jonah protested, describing his own harsh interpretation of her. I understood very soon that counseling had failed to address the couple's pattern of circular criticism. As smart and well-intentioned as they were, and even still professing their love for one another, after eighteen years they were exhausted from endless fighting over the same issues. To them these issues seemed insurmountable—their mutual criticism locking out any possibility for resolution.

What finally ended the cycle of criticism was when Jonah resisted the urge to "one-up" Carol and simply named his hurt feelings when she assigned a negative characteristic to him. "It hurts to hear you call me angry and mean. All I can think about is my dad who was *really* angry, *really* mean, and I am nothing like him." When Carol heard the honest distress in Jonah's statement, she paused and reassured him that he was nothing like his dad, a man whom she met when they first started dating. Jonah, now more assured that he was not the failure of a husband and father he began to suspect, was ready to take practical steps around managing his anger and lashing out.

In his book *Wired for Love*, Stan Tatkin, PsyD, says that our brains are fixed in a default setting that toggles between survival and winning.[2] In other words, we are more likely to attack or criticize than to defer a "win" to our loved ones. For this reason, he recommends that couples foster a "couple bubble" to counteract their natural tendency to war. Tatkin says the creation and consistent use of special couple words and behavior must reinforce safety and security, bonding, and attachment.

What is a couple-bubble? "Bubble" words and actions tell your partner that you nurture and protect them and have their back no matter what the circumstances. Yes, you guessed it, there is no room for criticism in a couple bubble.[3]

To create and promote a criticism-free relationship, Jonah and Carol needed to be clear on what criticism is and is not. We explored the differences between a critique, a complaint, and a request to change. It still took great effort, and there were missteps and apologies before the couple were clear of criticism in the form of words and body language, but they found their way into healthier forms of communication.

When Criticism Is Not Constructive

Criticism can enter your partner's vocabulary because they are dissatisfied with their own life. They may be a perfectionist on a mission to control, or a micromanager who is prone to being annoyed and frustrated. But even if your partner is expressing criticism specifically about your own behavior, sadly, your disapproving partner rarely gets what they want from statements like, "You always mess that up!" or "Why can't you ever remember to . . . " If you become aware that your partner communicates to you in this fashion, you must speak up as soon as possible in an effort to begin diagnosing the source of frustration your partner is experiencing.

The following story identifies how the relationship between Angie and Bob went downhill.

When Angie and Bob first met, so many elements aligned to make their relationship magical. Angie checked off Bob's list of wants and needs, and Bob soon won Angie's heart with romantic gestures and thoughtful actions. So, when Bob asked why she didn't grow her hair longer, or whether her choice of french fries was healthy, Angie quickly pushed down her hurt feelings without speaking up. Bob was fun to be with, after all; he eased the loneliness she faced in the past, and he was still the image of the guy she always wanted.

But the criticisms continued, and Angie's reactions strengthened. She lashed out at times, was defensive at others, and avoided certain food decisions when he was around. Worse, she grew ashamed of herself, guilty when she indulged, and she tried hard to change in other areas where he was critical. Others noticed Angie's personality change, sadness, and reclusiveness. Gone was the lighthearted woman they once knew.

Could Angie have spoken up about her needs and wants and changed the outcome? Maybe, if she had the right tools.

Nip It in the Bud

When a partner is faced with constant criticism from their significant other, the thought of how to address it might seem overwhelming or impossible. Hearing it so often, a partner might even start to believe that all of the other's critical comments are fair or simply true. But the key for the criticized partner is recognizing criticism as early as possible and working both within themselves and in teamwork with their partner to set a new course. The set of tips below provides a dependable, organized roadmap that any partner can follow to empower themselves when facing disproportionate or unproductive criticism from their partner.

Tip #1: Speak Up

When criticism first enters your partner's communication, it may be trivial and innocent, but if left unchecked, it has your permission to escalate. Ignoring criticism does you *both* harm as you neglect to find out what the core issue is and discuss how to solve your differences.

Instead, the criticism must be named, and the criticized partner must describe how it makes them feel. Only then can suggestions for change be made.

If allowed, criticism can be the beginning of the end of a relationship. Remember the cycle where one person criticizes, and the other defends? Such defense can take the form of righteous indignation or play out in the role of a defenseless victim. Both results are harmful in themselves but especially because nothing gets solved by them.

In his book *The Relationship Cure: A 5-Step Guide to Strengthening Your Marriage, Family, and Friendships*, aforementioned psychologist John Gottman explains that criticism leading to contempt is the most significant predictor of divorce.[4] You hear name-calling, insults, and meanness, but you worry that what lies beneath hurtful words and actions is your partner saying, "I am cleaner, smarter, more punctual, or better than you." Without intervention, contempt progresses, and withdrawal begins.

Emotional withdrawal, as we've previously referred to as "stonewalling," is an ineffective attempt to reduce conflict and eliminate hurt.

Examples of stonewalling include silence, turning away from the other person, refusing to answer questions, and speaking to the other person only indirectly. Unaddressed emotional withdrawal normally leads to the stonewalling partner finally moving out. All healthy relationships will have conflict as you are two different people. The answer is not to remain silent, suppressing your frustration, hurt, concern, and anger. It is to speak up using positive and respectful language that does not hurt. Here is an example of a defensive response that does not address the issue or the criticism at hand. The second example shows the criticism being confronted in a way that will allow the partners to engage in a helpful way.

Example 1 (Defensive): I can't do anything right in your eyes. You are so perfect! What if I am a little late from time to time?

Example 2 (Helpful): You've made a few sarcastic comments lately about my being late. It's hurtful. But I am willing to talk about how my lateness affects you and try to resolve it.

Tip #2: Set Boundaries.

As we've discussed, boundaries not only define who you are but equally express who you are *not*. Essential to a healthy, balanced lifestyle and happiness, boundaries are limitations, rules, or guidelines based on your own individual values, wants, and goals. Your boundaries provide you safety, and they ensure your freedom within any relationship.

If you do not express your boundaries to your partner, they will continue to expect you to act, make decisions, or conform to what they consider to be "the right way." They may have a "gold standard" mentality that says, "I know best," leading them to makes commands such as, "You should try for this job," "You should wear your hair this way," "You should eat this." Your partner may want to influence you, but when that desire crosses the line into personal matters that only you can decide, it is a violation of boundaries. This is the juncture at which acknowledging your autonomy and openly expressing your boundaries to your partner is so crucial. If you do not define your boundaries to your partner, they will continue to assume that their standards are your own and will criticize you for not conforming.

Tip #3: Keep Those Boundaries

As important as establishing and expressing your boundaries to your partner is, reiterating them *whenever necessary* is crucial. If you don't reinforce your limits, you will likely continue to face disrespect of your particular needs and preferences, but also honest and dishonest misunderstandings, a sense of entitlement on behalf of your partner, and even bullying. You must remember that your boundaries are not selfishly set, but necessary for promoting mutual respect between you and your partner. Consider these approaches to reinforcing your boundaries in a productive way.

You can explore your preferences, disagree, and still be loved: *Thanks for letting me vent about my colleagues and giving me advice. I won't leave my job just yet, though.*

You can say no without losing your partner: *A sailboat sounds like a lot of fun, but I don't want to spend my savings on one just yet.*

You can love and disagree with them: *I wish I liked my hair the way you want me to wear it. But I don't.*

And you can be yourself. Resist the desire to avoid criticism and to please at any cost. Set boundaries against insults, cursing, aggressive body language, and threats.

Tip #4: Aim for a 5:1 Ratio

Psychologist Gottman warns that couples need to expect from one another interactions that are five times more positive than negative, pointing out that people who are edging toward divorce have a ratio of 1:1 or less during conflict.[5] Sarcasm, complaints, judgment, and blame directed at your partner affect you both. Over time, the repeated script of negativity leaves you disappointed and hopeless about the relationship and less and less sure whether criticism from either end is actually false and unmerited. But if we consistently and conscientiously focus on the ways in which we interact with our partners, aiming to outweigh our conversations with intentionally positive statements and responses, we can begin to reverse the damage any thoughtless and self-interested criticism has caused.

Tip # 5: Don't Avoid Issues or Shift the Blame

While criticism is hurtful to you and harmful to your relationship, don't ignore the valid issues that motivate your partner to criticize you. You can acknowledge your partner's criticism in a measured way that does not reward their method of communication, but that ensures them that they are being heard and that you yourself are taking responsibility for your own actions. Along these lines, here is an example of how you might respond to your partner's concern about late payments owed by you on an account: *Late payments are a big deal. We need to fix that. I intend to make it a priority.* Additionally, make an effort, when necessary, to not excuse, rationalize, or justify any bad behavior on your part: *No excuse justifies my ignoring overdue bills.*

Tip# 6: Observe and Challenge Criticism Sandwiched with Positivity

Even if they are unaware they are doing it, a partner might subtly or blatantly frame their criticism of the other with seemingly positive statements, perhaps consciously or subconsciously making it easier for them to throw their hurtful barbs. By doing this they send confusing messages to the other:

"You know better than most how to make your point."

"You are so thoughtful at work, and everyone thinks the world of you . . . A different story at home."

However well-meaning or goal-oriented a partner's criticism may be, the criticism itself ultimately overrules the way in which it's packaged and will predictably result in damaging the other's self-esteem and your bond.

Tip # 7: Demonstrate to Others How You Should Be Treated

Due to childhood circumstances, many of us grow up believing we are unworthy of compassion and kindness, and we grow into our adulthood telling ourselves this very thing, allowing ourselves to absorb criticism from our partners in an unhealthy way. Learning to treat ourselves with compassion can often require the trained skills of a therapist, which I highly recommend if you find yourself feeling helpless in the face of a partner's criticism. In my previously mentioned session with the couple Jonah and Carol, who had found themselves unable to escape a cycle of criticism and unhealthy responses, I learned that Jonah spent his childhood trying and failing to please his angry and critical father. It was Carol who provided the heartbreaking details of a father who ridiculed Jonah's fumbles on the playing field, failures at school, and inability to stand up for himself the way his brothers did. Though Jonah is today a sought-after physician, he treated himself the way his father did so many years ago. It was as if he had taken a photograph of his father's voice, tone, and expressions and superimposed it on the image of who he truly was. Psychologists call this the "internalized parent." The truly poignant part of Jonah and Carol's story, and that of so many other couples, is that the wounded-child-grown-into-adulthood had hoped that their partner would be the "one" to see them as worthy. In his romance with Carol, Jonah couldn't initially see how Carol's criticism actually reminded him of his father's during his childhood. Ultimately, Jonah took the important lesson to treat himself with the love and respect he wanted others to give him.

You can solve relationship problems without criticism. The following examples describe healthy and unhealthy ways to deal with criticism and the related relationship destroyers of defensiveness, contempt, or stonewalling.

Negative Responses	Positive Alternatives
Criticism focuses on the other person's faults and diminishes them by the implicit suggestion that their personality is inadequate. *You've left a mess for me to clean up again! Living with you is a chore.*	Use "I" statements to express your feelings, identify your needs, and achieve your goal. A gentle tone and neutral body language help to preserve the connection with your partner. Correction: *I believe I do my share of the cleaning. Can we make a plan to divide the chores fairly?*
Defensiveness is harmful because it relieves one partner of responsibility and stymies problem-solving, creating the dynamic of offense-defense. Defensiveness often ends in frustration, a fight, or withdrawal. *I would have cleaned it up. It wasn't that bad!*	Listening carefully and taking responsibility for the truth in an accusation is the best response. You don't have to agree that you were completely in the wrong, if this is the case. *I could have cleaned up right away. Can we make time to revisit our responsibilities?*
Contempt is the expression of superiority from one to another. It may come in the form of sarcasm, hostility, eye-rolling, or sneering. Contempt deeply impacts the other's self-esteem. *I am cleaning up after you again! You are so lazy!*	The health of your relationship depends on eradicating all contempt. We can eradicate contempt by paying closer attention to and openly empathizing with our partner's experience and needs. *I can see that you are tired when you get home. Can we talk about finding a good time to do chores?*

Stonewalling is the withdrawal from conflict primarily through frustration, the belief that you are incapable of solving a problem, and emotional burnout.

I ask you to clean up over and over again with no change. I'm done talking about it.

When one person becomes frustrated, partners must call a timeout to exit the conversation and engage in a calming, distracting activity that works to rebuild a bond and renew energies.

A timeout is not a copout when you commit as a team to returning to your discussion. Setting a concrete time to do so will help partners follow through.

I am feeling overwhelmed. Can we take a break to cook together, and then get back to this immediately after supper?

Reflection | Day 9:
Dealing with Criticism from Your Partner

Points to Remember
Criticism breaks relationships. Avoid lashing out, defensiveness, or ignoring the problem at hand. Instead, be assertive and focus as a team on problem-solving.

Questions to Consider
Are you calm, friendly, and sincere when you're being assertive? Or do you think you communicate your feelings in an overly emotional or indifferent way?

Action Plan
Find helpful ways to address criticism. Use these examples as a guide for healthy responses:

I was upset when you made fun of my outfit. I prefer that you tell me privately when you don't like my clothes.

Describing me as a drama queen is hurtful. In the future, let's talk about what I do and say that makes you uncomfortable.

Making a face when you come home doesn't clean the house. It just makes me overwhelmed. Why don't we work together on a solution?

Practice a gentle start to your response that identifies your partner's criticism, say plainly how it makes you feel, and make suggestions on how your partner can rephrase.

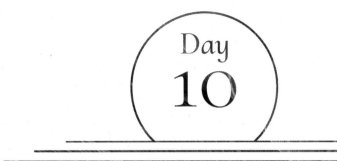

Addressing Your Own Critical Nature

Is this familiar?

You don't want to hurt your significant other, or yourself, and you especially don't want to damage your relationship. Yet, your habit of criticism returns despite your best efforts. Is it that you *just have* to make your point? Feel inauthentic when you stay silent? Or believe there is no other way of getting what you need except to criticize?

On Day 9 you dealt with criticism from your partner and learned how to respond to them. Day 10 speaks to the critical partner, helps them understand why they overreact with criticism and the effects of their criticism, and makes suggestions on how to transform their methods of communication.

It is hard to live with someone who is laid back and happy-go-lucky when you are cautious, anxious, or excitable by nature; or with someone who manages time loosely when you are a stickler for being early. You and your significant other may have differing perspectives on cleanliness, on budgeting, on how children should be parented and how families should behave—and all the while, the question nags you: to criticize or not to criticize? But you feel unequipped to take an alternative approach to communicating your frustrations, having never learned the rules of engagement that make a relationship last.

Meanwhile, the criticism you unleash on your partner can range from subtle hints of displeasure to overt expressions; it is sometimes disguised in "friendly sarcasm," generalized complaints, and negative body language. One thing, however, is for sure: as long as it sends a clear message of disapproval, your significant other feels the sting.

As dramatic as it sounds, we must remember that criticism damages on a catastrophic scale, as its perpetuation predicts a sequence of events that lead to divorce, as John Gottman's studies have shown. In my own clinical experience, criticism is often the first big disappointment that couples face in a love relationship.

We can see the damaging effects of criticism in the story of Kaitlin and Drew.

After an exciting courtship, marriage, and two children, Kaitlin and Drew were in my office to discuss Drew's criticism of Kaitlin's housecleaning, parenting, and personality traits. After their glorious beginnings, she now avoided the Sunday-afternoon brunch with his super-tidy family as often as possible and dreaded the last-minute housecleaning when she heard his car in the driveway. Drew never actually called Kaitlin "sloppy" or "dirty," but his expressions and body language sent that message as clearly as any words he could otherwise say.

When Kaitlin tried to address his criticism of her, the conversations ended with all the reasons they needed to keep a clean house and protect their investment, and to teach their children good habits. She kept trying harder, but Drew continued to find all the spots she missed. Kaitlin was ready to exit and find a place she could cook, clean, and co-parent away from Drew's critical eye.

In another counseling appointment, Drew asked, "When is the right time to solve problems? And what about the issues that don't get solved?" He believed that problems needed to be solved *right away*, while Kaitlin needed time away from the issues. To his credit, Drew was committed to a relationship free from criticism, and this certainly meant solving problems and asking for change. The truth is, the right time for Drew and Kaitlin could've been later, or could've been now—*as long as they both agreed.*

The immediate problem for Drew, however, was that the only way he knew how to solve his problems with Kaitlin *now* was through expressing anger through criticism.

A couple doesn't need to separate to learn a new way of communicating and managing their lives. Drew and Kaitlin eventually renegotiated their needs, resulting in a career change that didn't demand late nights at the office, and she resumed work she enjoyed. They spent their evenings dividing the tasks of home and care for their children while making time for date nights and adventure—the very activities that brought them together at the beginning of their romance.

Exploring the Origins of Your Critical Nature

There are many reasons why adults become critical creatures. It can be learned behavior, an ego defense, or a reaction fueled by fear. You may have grown up in a home where criticism was the norm, and despite a decision not to invoke the same negative feelings in others, that style of messaging has become your default response.

Your critical nature may not be the result of your experiences in your upbringing or early life, but a reflection of your present internal struggles. For instance, when you criticize your partner, you may in fact be responding in fear, jealousy, insecurity, or guilt as you recognize in their own behavior something true about yourself that you'd wish to deny or ignore. You may be recognizing something that makes you aware of your own hidden desires or inclinations. In other words, your own criticism might be motivated by an urge toward self-protection, even if the result is the opposite. But here, only a healthy practice of self-reflection can help you recognize these modes of response.

Let's consider the following example of overreaction and criticism in my clients Damon and Deb.

Damon and Deb are stuck in a pattern of his criticism and her hurt and, since he does not recognize and address his ongoing negative feelings—in this case his fear—the cycle never ceases. Damon is triggered when Deb is late from work, takes on activities outside the home, or spends time with friends. He lashes out, saying, "You are always late. What keeps you at work an extra hour? You leave me to pick up the kids and start supper. You've got it easy."

We can only imagine the hurt and negativity that Deb feels after this attack. Or Damon's distress at her counterattack or withdrawal. The truth is, Damon may be embarrassed to admit his worry that she doesn't love him as much, and that he feels rushed without her help. However, that admission would move the couple closer to a solution.

What if Damon had said, "It's hard to get everything done when you aren't here. Besides, I am worried you don't enjoy being with me as much as with your friends."

We must remember:

Our criticism doesn't change our partner's bad habits.

Our criticism doesn't make our partner believe we are right.

Our criticism causes our partner to resent us.

What *does* occur from our relentless criticism is that soon enough all our partner hears in our voice are the signs and sounds of attack and negativity, and all of our otherwise positive traits may gradually become invisible to them. Simultaneously, our partner suffers from growing insecurity and a sense of unworthiness, possibly leading to chronic depression.

If you are a critical partner, the first steps toward repairing your relationship begins with you as much as it does your partner—and it depends on, as always, a real conversation.

Solutions Start with a Conversation

If you are a critical partner, your goal is to have *productive* conversations with your significant other, but the first step to achieve this is to openly acknowledge your awareness of your critical nature, openly recognize the harm it causes, and together, admit that your criticism and your partner's responses to it have created a rift in your bond together. This key action opens the doors for four remaining steps for conversation: talking about your differences, agreeing to solve problems together, requesting behavior change, and setting an intention to continue handling occasional relapses together. Let's consider the five steps more deeply.

Step 1: Acknowledging Your Critical Nature

Admitting to your critical nature and its harm to your partner is especially difficult because it takes humility and willingness to forgive yourself. Admitting as a couple that your relationship is damaged is equally challenging, since it is difficult to acknowledge together that things are not as they were in the beginning of your romance. But remember that the door to the remaining steps in your conversation cannot be opened without shared acknowledgment.

Step 2: Talk about Your Differences

As previously explored, all couples naturally have many differences. One may be more time-aware, tidier, or have less tolerance for noise. Another may have a different parenting style or different weekend interests. Name and describe these differences to each other, and then make a habit of reassessing them over time. Acknowledging how your differences affect *each of you* allows yourself as a critical partner to feel as if you're conversing on a level playing field. It is then important to agree on discussing your differences over time in the spirit of continually making adjustments for one another. This agreement will help each of you continue to enjoy and grow through life together as unique individuals.

Step 3: Agree to Solve Problems Together

Keeping the focus on solving issues, and doing so as a team, will naturally tamp down on the impulse to blame and criticize. The time you spend with your partner naming your problems, brainstorming solutions, and coming to resolutions together will simply replace the time spent in negative criticism/response cycles. Remember that the key to solving problems together is broaching topics in a conscientious and cooperative way: "I've noticed that the bills sometimes get missed. Can we discuss a system for paying bills on time?"

Step 4: Request Behavior Change

You've acknowledged your differences with your partner and you've made a pact to solve your problems together. As a critical partner, now is the time to request behavior change on behalf of your significant other in a productive way. Here are four rules to request behavior change:

1. Use specific examples to describe your grievance.
2. Describe how the issue affects you: "When the bills are overdue, I feel like our life is falling apart, and that we are failing. It reminds me of the worries I had as a child."
3. Make a specific request that focuses on changing the issue, not the person: "Are you willing to make two meals each week so I can handle the budget and pay the bills?" "I would like to automate our bill payments. How do you feel about that?"
4. Have no expectations. A request is not a demand. It trades on the mutual desire to be an effective community where each partner is ultimately happy.

Your significant other wants you to be open, honest, and share your needs, and now you know you can do it without criticism. Continue to review the following examples of critical statements and alternative requests for behavior change, using these as a model for practicing until the alternative approach becomes more natural to you.

Criticism (accusatory): Why do you leave the kitchen in such a mess?

Request for behavior change (calm and measured): Susan, can you please remember to clean the kitchen when you make a meal? I feel overwhelmed when this room is messy.

Criticism (aggressive): You always leave the kitchen a mess!

Request for behavior change (future-focused and inclusive): I would like us to make an effort to keep the kitchen counter clean. I enjoy the house when there is some order.

Criticism (shaming): You are such a messy person!

Request for behavior change (acknowledging strengths and encouraging): I have seen how organized and tidy your office is and trust we can make an effort to keep the rest of the house tidy.

Criticism (problem-focused): It is awful to come home to a messy house.

Request for behavior change (promoting collaboration): I know we can work together to clean and tidy our home.

Step 5: Handle Relapses Together

A commitment to change is never automatic, nor does it always follow a predictable, consistent path toward improvement. Your best intentions and efforts will fail if you aren't diligent in keeping each other accountable in your journey to be noncritical. Catch your critical self in the act, apologize, and rephrase.

Reflection | Day 10:
Addressing Your Own Nature to Criticize

Points to Remember
If unacknowledged, your criticism of your partner can have irreparable effects. Fortunately, you can adjust how you communicate your frustration with your partner through thoughtful requests and goal-oriented, mutually beneficial conversations.

Questions to Consider
Where did your critical nature originate? What steps will you take to examine it and transform it into something better for both your partner *and* you?

Action Plan
Be a detective of your own nature as you work on changing your mode of communication from critical to encouraging.

Consider using index cards as tools to list your partner's assets, as well as noticeable improvements and contributions to your relationship. Then, share the cards with your partner in order to acknowledge them and directly compliment them.

Continue this exercise as you notice mutual admiration, respect, and love rebuilding between you and your partner.

The Three Dos and Don'ts of Problem-Solving

Is this familiar?

You have just failed to have a successful conversation with your partner, and you think to yourself, "We are stuck before we begin."

If you feel like you are constantly hitting a brick wall when trying to have conversations with your partner, or your discussions lead to fights but no solutions, it could be that what you need is to learn new relationship tools for problem-solving. Day 11 lays all these tools on the table.

Problem-solving is an important skill to have in any situation, but it is one that is not intuitive to most people. I have heard the words "I hate confrontation" often enough to believe that most of us are truly averse to disagreement—that is, allergic to ideas that are different from ours and avoidant of any situation that inspires anger in ourselves or others. I confess that I have felt an aversion to discord myself, that I have resorted to twisting and changing my beliefs just to avoid arguments. Don't misunderstand, there is nothing wrong with changing illogical beliefs, but avoiding dialogue is the worst way to be in a relationship.

Marc and Lorne are an example of a couple who had swept so much under the rug, there was barely enough space for them in the same room. Marc was the only child of a single mother who created a safe haven for his creativity, while Lorne was from a rule-driven religious background that continued to direct his beliefs about "the right way." It was no surprise that the couple were at odds with issues around money, friends, and extended family and dealt with these differences in a cycle of avoidance/politeness and occasional blowouts.

Their conflict-based conversations often started with, "You always," or "Why can't you?" and were paired with expressions of frustration, anger, and even hints of disgust. The typical response between these partners was defensiveness and shock that escalated to hurtful words, silence, and withdrawal, or a quick apology followed by retreat. But the issues at hand—that of Marc's spending and his tendency to forget obligations—were not solved.

It was indeed a blowout that brought the couple to a counseling appointment. They couldn't actually remember what they fought about that day but still felt the sting of the barbed conversation in their memory.

"How can we walk back from this?" Marc had asked with hurt in his voice. My response was to ask the couple to agree to the following five foundations of dealing with differences and adhere to the recommended dos and don'ts of problem-solving.

Change your mindset about differences. All couples have differences, and there is no such thing as a conflict-free relationship, so we need to view conflicts as a normal part of a couple's life. When we don't vent our disagreements, they percolate and become little volcanoes, having missed their opportunity to be quelled through cooperation and agreement.

Solve problems as they arise. As urged before, you must *speak up* about your relationship concerns as they arise and commit to working with your partner toward a solution. When you can't find a solution quickly, continue to make it a priority as long as the concern persists.

Stay with one issue at a time. Pay close attention to the exact issues your partner is bringing up and make every effort to manage your emotions to stay focused on and respond thoughtfully to the issue at hand.

Listen and avoid interruptions. The space you give to your partner to allow them to think and speak is key to handling your differences and solving problems. Make sure to patiently listen, making mental notes when you feel compelled to interrupt.

Equal treatment. Give the same consideration to your partner's point of view as you would to your own. Remind yourself that you are on the same side as them and that the goal is to win together.

Struggles around sex, in-laws, parenting, shifting values, and disrespect are only a few examples of problems that can undermine a relationship. The fact is, these are not unsolvable or insurmountable except when left to fester. As a therapist, I have watched couples avoid, withdraw, attack each other, or become so hurt and angry at everyday challenges that they neglect the task of solving them. As a result, the pain of these difficulties persists. Once you understand the importance of problem-solving and are ready to follow its best practices, there are actions you can take. That leads to the don'ts. And the dos.

The Three Don'ts of Problem-Solving

You and your partner may intend to become more and more mindful of the five foundations for dealing with differences, but progress here can be swiftly reversed if the "don'ts" of problem-solving are not minded as well. Let's review each of them in detail.

Don't Avoid the Problem

Perhaps it was a minor incident, a sarcastic comment, a frustrated expression, or something more significant. You don't like to fight. You worry that you'll open up a risky topic. You worry that you might hurt the other person—so, your instinct is to ignore the problem and let sleeping dogs lie.

Not all attempts at problem-solving—at least first attempts—can be assured to be successful, but the benefit of dealing with issues when they are *small* far outweighs the cost of waiting years to address a problem that has grown to unmanageable proportions. Meanwhile, when you solve a problem in collaboration with your partner, it only strengthens your commitment and bond to one another. A shared sigh of relief is felt in the reinvigorated promise of your relationship.

Don't Withdraw

We've talked about the problem of withdrawal in a broad sense and also specifically in regards to how we might respond to criticism. It is equally crucial to be aware of and avoid our impulse toward withdrawal once we have agreed with our partners to enter the problem-solving stage.

It is tempting to walk away angry and hurt when a solution isn't obvious. A handy alternative is agreeing to a delay. A delay allows each partner to pause and manage their emotions, to gather more information, and to thoughtfully prepare for further conversation and negotiation.

Feeling compelled to withdraw also presents a good opportunity to practice, as previously suggested, releasing all expectations and shift your focus on understanding your partner as far as their feelings and their needs. Ask for details, listen more carefully, and let each other know how much you appreciate their perspective. Do this for as long as needed and enjoy the byproduct of caring about another's point of view. If the issue is critical and requires an immediate solution, agree on a temporary one that you can revisit later.

Don't Permit Excessive Emotions and Harsh Rhetoric

Harsh and hurtful rhetoric begins with poorly moderated emotions. As listening, asking questions, and negotiating are the friends of healthy problem-solving in a relationship, harsh and hurtful rhetoric are its enemies, reversing any progress previously made. Meanwhile, a distraught or angry person can take center stage, becoming the primary issue and leaving the original problem languishing.

Three Dos of Problem-Solving

Simply think of the three "dos" of problem-solving as the exact opposite of the three don'ts. That is, the opposite of deferring to avoidance, withdrawal, excessive emotions, and harsh rhetoric is peaceful and thoughtful engagement with your partner, followed by mutual dedication to a well-organized strategy to begin assessing and addressing the problem at hand.

Do Gently Lead-In

Focusing on being relaxed and gentle at the problem-solving stage helps you open and manage the conversation. This kind of nonthreatening environment counteracts stress, prevents the triggering of either partner, and helps to keep each partner's attention on the problem at hand.

Examine the following exchange where one partner confronts his significant other's look of frustration, but then follows up by inquiring into her well-being, building rapport and assuring her he is committed to helping solve the issue at hand.

> **John:** "I see your look of frustration. Are you still angry about my mother?"
> **Claire:** "No. I am sad, that's all."
> **John:** "That makes sense. She was out of line. Is there something I can do?"
> **Claire:** "I am not sure."
> **John:** "If you think of something I have missed, let me know. Let's keep talking about it until we come up with a solution."

Aforementioned researcher John Gottman has observed that the first three minutes of a couple's conflict conversation predicts what will happen in a couple's relationship.[1] If said couple's dispute is left unsolved, we can expect the predictions of the three-minute conversation to prove themselves years later into their relationship.

The success of the first three minutes of any couple's problem-solving conversation is wholly dependent upon each partner leading into the discussion with a concern for being gentle with their partner. To recall Marc and Lorne, they found themselves hindered by initiating conversations in the spirit of anger and frustration with accusatory statements beginning with "Why do you . . ." and "You always . . . " But they worked on transforming their lead-ins into gentle, sincere, clarification-seeking statements that set a proper foundation for following up with requests.

I am curious about the comment you made about my parents . . .

I am concerned you believe my parents are to blame . . .

I notice you have been shopping . . .

It's important to me that you can relax more . . .

Gentle lead-ins establish rapport, reinforce the warmth of connection, and prevent negativity from guiding the dialogue. If a couple can maintain a gentle-minded tone throughout a conversation, they are more likely to sustain balance and reach agreement.

Do Stay Calm

In the context of problem-solving conversations, we can think of calmness as the older sibling of the gentle lead-in. Partners might successfully enter a problem-solving conversation with gentle lead-ins, but the groundwork this lays can be quickly pulverized if each partner cannot moderate their emotions, even when upsetting topics or opinions enter the discourse. When we are in a fearful, aggressive, or agitated state, our limbic systems initiate the fight-or-flight response, urging us toward acrimony and withdrawal—in other words, hindering us from being able to solve problems creatively by keeping the big picture in mind and applying the skills we have otherwise learned. Nonetheless, let us remember that if there are signs our gentle lead-ins will be sabotaged by uncontrolled emotions on either partner's behalf at the start of a problem-solving conversation, we are allowed to call a "time-out" in order to cool off, regain an objective perspective, and return later to the conversation in a productively empathetic and goal-oriented mindset.

It was difficult for Marc and Lorne to appreciate that it is possible to stay calm, that they were not slaves to their hot tempers, and that they did not have to be forever imprisoned in the learned behavior they had witnessed in their own families. Marc had once commented that his family of origin was loud—but that it was also loving, and it worked for them. While I acknowledged this, I took the opportunity here to make a comparison of a couple's out-of-control argument to an airplane making a crash-landing. When an airplane is on its way to a crash-landing, I explained, the pilot asks you to put on an oxygen mask, not because it prevents the airplane from crashing but because it helps you breathe and take the next steps. Without a reasonable state of calm on behalf of each partner, couples don't have the "oxygen" to think critically and come to an agreement on how to move forward when a problem-solving conversation is appearing to go off the rails.

Calmness gives partners the clarity of mind to listen, respond, and validate each other in a way that prioritizes true understanding and resolution. Calmness also gives us the strength to attend to our partner when they find themselves responding with excessive emotions during conversation. We feel able to be patient, to plant a peace flag in the current conversation, and to give all our attention over to our significant other, whether in the form of empathetic silence or the physical gesture of a handhold or a hug. Calmness allows us to slow the world down and quell fires threatening to rage out of control.

Do Agree on a Tried-and-True Problem-Solving Plan

Gentle initiations and emotional moderation provide a platform over which a solid, mutually organized problem-solving plan of action can be written. Such a plan, written with clear rules of engagement, helps to maintain a level playing field beneath each partner.

When creating a problem-solving plan, partners must first openly acknowledge that, while several problems might be voiced, *not all problems can be solved at once.*

Lorne and Marc, anxious as they were to have a good long-term relationship, also needed to learn that relationships are not a scientific equation or a jigsaw puzzle with all the pieces present, just waiting to be organized; that problems need to be talked about, but each individual problem needs its own time and process to resolve. The couple also needed to accept that, in any relationship, some problems will never be fully solved, but that such problems can be continually mitigated through acceptance, empathy, and big-picture thinking.

143

An effective problem-solving plan hinges on four requirements:
1. Dedicating a plan to one identified problem only.
2. Working with your partner to clearly define your plan.
3. Thinking in terms of "We," and not "I."
4. Sequencing your plan by starting with problem recognition and ending in an agreed-upon method to address and resolve the problem.

The basic structure to follow for writing out a problem-solving plan is as follows:

Problem (Ensuring mutual understanding)
Our problem is that . . .
Discuss Solutions to Problem (Brainstorming multiple ideas)
To solve our problem, we will . . .
Stay Focused on the Problem (Pausing and regrouping)
If we lose focus on the problem, we will . . .
Maintaining Healthy Behavior (Maintaining focus on partner)
To listen carefully to each other, we will . . .
To make sure we're treating each other as equals, we will . . .
Selecting a Solution (Planning together)
Let's begin with approach A and reconvene to make changes as needed.
Evaluating success (Making adjustments together)
Perhaps the most important step we can make is to decide what parts of a solution are working and what are not.

Meanwhile, you may add additional prompts for consideration, as many as you find helpful. You and your partner should also feel free to return to any step in problem-solving and revise wherever necessary. Perhaps you've realized you did not originally define your problem as clearly as you could have. Perhaps you've discovered an even better way for one another to regain focus on your problem when it begins to fade. The key is to remember to always work together as a team on your problem-solving plan, never making revisions without your partner's awareness and consensus.

Reflection | Day 11:
The Three Dos and Don'ts of Problem-Solving

Points to Remember
Unsolved problems leave an elephant in the room and pave the way for unproductive emotions and behavior.

Questions to Consider
In your own relationship, what is stopping you and your partner from solving your problems?

Action Plan
Prioritize writing a problem-solving plan with your partner, making sure that you are using "We," rather than "I," statements. Feel free to continue to adapt your plan, especially by adding additional statements you both think will help you view your relationship objectively and understand it on a deeper level.

The Stubborn Problem

Is this familiar?

"We just can't get past our differences," you find yourself telling a friend. "This problem has lasted for so long, I don't think it'll ever go away."

I agree that some problems are just stubborn. Day 12 helps you understand how to handle problems that continue to appear unsolvable.

Every relationship goes through times of trouble. For you, it might feel that the issues you are facing with your partner are worse than everyone else's. But in reality, the problems you are tackling may not be as unique and as complicated as you believe.

There is even research to back that up. In a 2011 study of 108 couples, relationship challenges spread evenly overall into three main categories: issues with communication, emotional affection, and physical affection, including sex.[1] This is in line with what I witness in couples therapy and in my own relationships. Most problems we face fall into these broad categories. Though serious, they are not insurmountable.

In your relationship you may be currently asking yourself, "What do I do when my partner refuses to change?" or "Why does this keep happening between us?" This is the time to pause and invite your partner to a conversation where you both consider if either or both of you are experiencing one of these core issues:

- A violation of someone's values
- A power struggle
- An out-of-balance ego
- An unrealistic expectation

Often, it is one of these core issues that is the root of a stubborn problem. Let's consider how each of these issues can be addressed productively.

Understand and Affirm Your Significant Other's Values

Our values are the bedrock for our perceptions of the world and our beliefs as to how to live within it—without them, life is simply meaningless. When each of us feels as if we're living by our values, we experience joy and a sense of purpose. Humans tend to share the same topics when it comes to our values, regardless of the differences of our values themselves. Values tend to revolve around the subjects of personal freedom, health and wellness, service to others, fun and adventure, home and family, and love and compassion. Sometimes it takes us well into adulthood to really discover what our true values are.

Meanwhile, most couples cannot claim that they share perfectly equal values, and eventually the discrepancy can cause pain and suffering if not addressed in a healthy and goal-oriented manner.

You may have experienced a time in your relationship when a disagreement blossomed into a hurtful argument in which your partner confusingly seemed unwilling to compromise, could not seem to listen to logic, or was fixated on a past wrong you once committed. There even seemed to be an unspoken subtext to the argument that your partner refused to voice or seemed to not quite be able to find the words to express. In this case, it is possible that you have struck the bedrock of your partner's values, values that were conflicting with your own in relation to the topic at hand.

It is not realigning your values to match your partner's that is the solution to the above scenario, but rather coming to respect and even cherish the unique values of your partner, showing them that you truly "get who they are." You should expect the same from your partner in the shared understanding that this is the only way to coexist with one another in the long-term.

John and Claire's story is an example of a couple staying connected despite being nagged by a stubborn problem. Over the course of several weeks, John and Claire were visited by John's mother—who prides herself on being direct and speaking her mind—on several occasions. During each visit, Claire noticed John's mother passive-aggressively commenting on her parenting style, quality of housework, and approach to her career as she found things to subtly criticize about their house. Claire was especially distraught about John's silence in the face of these potshots. Meanwhile, John noticed over these weeks Claire becoming distant and cold with him. He grew more and more confused when she would refuse to sit close, go to bed at their usual time, or sleep or laugh together. When he asked Claire what was wrong, she would say nothing, but he knew things weren't right.

Once John realized there might be something deeper going on, he began asking Claire different questions.

"Thinking about it now, when my mother said, 'Women these days,' I can tell it hit a nerve. What did you hear?" John asked.

Claire said, "It was like she was making a direct attack on me, telling me I didn't care about the house or our kids as much as I actually do. And you just sat beside her with a pleasant expression that suggested agreement."

"I could see how hurtful that was, and with me not speaking up too. I know you are an effective and excellent parent."

John realized that he did not place as much value on Claire's sense of well-being as a parent as he should have; but the more John validated (truthfully) Claire's parenting, the more quickly she returned to her old self.

In the case above, breached values showed their face in the form of extreme emotions, and uncharacteristic behavior, resulting in deep confusion on behalf of the other partner. It was only when John stopped to thoughtfully inquire as to why Claire was so upset that he discovered that her values had been challenged. It was at this point that he became able to not only acknowledge her values, but affirm them. It can be argued that acknowledging and affirming the values of your partner that are *different* from your own is exceedingly more critical than doing so for your shared values, as this action reinforces the relationship bond against something that could otherwise produce a sense of insecurity and distance between the two of you.

Even if you have a different parenting style than you partner, you can still tell them, "You are the most thoughtful parent and friend I know."

Even if you feel differently about the role and meaning of work in life, you can still tell your partner, "I respect and support your drive to succeed at work."

Even if you are interested in different causes and concerned about different problems in the world, you can still tell your partner, "The world is a better place because you care."

And even if you have some personality differences with your partner, you can still reassure them that "I wouldn't be the person I am without your fun-loving nature."

In the Action Plan for this chapter, you will find a game that you can play with your partner to help each of you discover and better understand each other's values. The game will require thoughtful questioning, careful listening, and collaborative analysis.

End a Power Struggle

Sometimes a stubborn problem stems from one partner's desire to be right, to "win" at all times. This mindset makes it hard to see the other's point of view, ensuring that conversations will not be collaborative attempts at solutions but rather struggles for power. Meanwhile, the other partner might suppress their preferences and personality to keep the peace for the winning-minded partner. We now know that this kind of intentional suppression on behalf of one partner can lead to frustration, resentment, and withdrawal.

Competition is hardwired in all of us due to our survival instinct; in modern life it helps us excel in activities such as sports, school, and work. But permitting this instinct to dictate our behavior in our relationships can only result in a significant other feeling like—or actually becoming—a "loser." The cost of the winning partner's triumph can only be the negation of the other's values and point of view, and a closing off of empathy and compassion for them—all resulting in a catastrophic loosening of the relationship bond. As long as one partner holds onto a win-lose mentality, healthy negotiation and problem-solving are off the table.

Check Your Ego

Your relationship might be stuck in a stubborn problem because you or your partner's ego is in the way.

What is ego essentially? It is who you believe you are and are not, at times showing itself like a billboard in our defensive gestures and expressions when we are in disagreement with our partners. When we have an "unchecked" ego, we are led by arrogance, insecurity, and a persistent sense of righteousness.

While we all have an ego, we don't have to erase it for the sake of our partner; we just need to keep it in balance. Simultaneously, we need to strengthen ourselves to feel secure enough to set our egos aside in order to help us see eye to eye with our partners.

If you or your partner are allowing yourselves to be ruled by an unchecked ego, resulting in your stubbornly holding on to your point of view, continually justifying your position, always searching for "proof" you are right, then it's time for you to relax your own position, at least for the moment. Temporarily releasing your grip on your point of view is not giving up, nor is it giving in to your partner's perspective; rather, it is a choice to solve your relationship problem without interference from the "third person," the unbalanced ego. This may not result in you or your partner's ability to see the other's perspective with total clarity, but it will help you to mindfully listen to one another in a genuinely curious and objective way, thereby laying the path to finally unravel a stubborn problem.

Think of your stubborn problem as the rope in a tug of war. In this game, two teams pull at opposite ends of a rope until one overpowers the other and carries them over a central line. When you release your tight grip on your own point of view and let go of the metaphorical rope, the other person finds themselves off-balance and may then be compelled to loosen their own tight grip on their point of view.

The following examples highlight how our thinking changes after we check our egos and relax our grip on our locked-in perspectives:

Partner 1 is upset that Partner 2 doesn't want to attend church services with them on Sundays.
Partner 2: I'm just not interested in going.
Partner 1 (Ego-Ruled Response): You are disrespectful to a religious practice that is important to me.
Partner 1 (Checked-Ego Response): I understand you're not interested in attending church with me. Is there a specific reason why? Is there something spiritual or fulfilling you would like to do together at other times instead?

Partner 1 is responding to Partner 2's being upset that they constantly leave a backyard gate unlocked.
Partner 1: Why are you so upset about the gate?
Partner 2 (Ego-Ruled Response): Because you don't care about how important the safety of our house is to me.
Partner 2 (Checked-Ego Response): I'm also concerned about safety. Is there a reason that it's helpful to you to keep the gate unlocked? Can we talk about finding a different solution to help you enter and exit the backyard more easily?

Each non-egotistic answer illustrates one partner loosening their grip on their insecurity and dilutes the ego's arrogance that is keeping a stubborn problem from breaking through the gates of resolution. As with our discussion of values, the suggested game in this chapter's Action Plan includes an exercise on analyzing our egos.

Be Realistic with Your Expectations of Each Other

We've discussed the importance of managing and even eliminating our expectations when seeking behavior change in our partners. It is equally important to understand that sometimes we must release our expectations that a specific problem can be solved entirely at all, and that part of being in a relationship is learning to compromise with your significant other on certain issues.

It's important to continually remind ourselves that every relationship has unsolvable problems, and even that similar problems are sometimes weighed differently across different relationships. What is a big issue in my relationship may be insignificant in yours, and vice versa. You may exit one relationship because of its challenges and meet someone new, only to discover a brand-new issue that is equally frustrating. That is why it is rarely wise to leave a partner because you are not perfectly compatible or synchronized—at least not without having tried to meet in the middle.

Let's consider Julie, who learned this very lesson when she ended her relationship with Zack.

Julie wanted Zack to be more patient and understanding when she withdrew from work and friends, grieving the loss of a parent. But, although supportive and thoughtful, Zack was more solution-focused and misunderstood the grieving process. When he asked her to explain her feelings, she was shocked that he didn't "just know." Without much explanation she left their life together and met someone new.

The relationship Julie started six months later with Alex, however, ended after just two years because she felt he was unreliable and irresponsible. Julie then took some time out for soul-searching before getting into another relationship. After some time, she felt she had found "the One" in Maurice. She carefully selected him, seeing in him the right blend of assertive and relaxed. However, after eight years together Julie found herself faced with his unbending decision of never wanting to get married and have children.

After these disappointments, Julie reflected and openly admitted that she missed Zack and that it would have been wiser to have worked with him to solve their misunderstanding.

All couples will face differences and disagreements, but these might turn into stubborn problems when they're deepened by unrealistic expectations on either partner's behalf. The lingering disappointment that ensues might show itself in diminished sexual desire, occasional boredom, or lingering bad habits that don't take a partner into account. In the case of Zack, Julie eventually learned that she had been overfocusing on the behavior of Zack's that bothered her while not taking the step to open up a conversation with him in order to work their way toward compromise. Julie knew that she could've reconsidered what she was actually expecting from Zack and whether or not it was truly reasonable.

As partners we must learn to catch ourselves when we begin to form negative beliefs about the other because they are not meeting our expectations, as often these beliefs do not represent the absolute truth. When we decide that "he's lazy" or "she doesn't care," we may indeed be making a false assumption about the true intentions of our significant other. Meanwhile, the stubborn problem wrought by our misunderstanding leads us to overly focus on the 10 percent about our partners that frustrate us, and not the 90 percent that brings us joy.

The Two Parts of a Stubborn Problem: Problem A and Problem B

The common denominator between all of these core issues that feed stubborn problems is how partners treat one another when trying to seek understanding and come to a resolution.

The stubborn problem itself is Problem A. When partners communicate with one another in unproductive and harmful ways, this is Problem B. In our relationships, we must always first address Problem B in order to solve Problem A.

In the following example, we'll observe how a couple eventually finds themselves capable of productively discussing their Problem A only after committing to patience, listening deeply, and acknowledging each other's needs:

Elam is shy, but she tries hard to be outgoing at work, so much so that when Tom arrives home in the evening after his commute, she feels depleted and seeks solitude. Meanwhile, Tom wants to share his every thought and idea, as well as his hobbies, with Elam. Tom's ongoing sense of Elam's absence makes him feel lost and unloved.

Initially, Elam and Tom only argued in after-work conversations, him accusing her of ignoring him and not devoting any time or energy to his interests or spending time together in general; her accusing him of ignoring her as well, and not respecting the time she needs for herself after work.

Soon Elam and Tom became exhausted in the stream of unproductive arguing and, with a new clarity of mind, they decided to "start the conversation over," agreeing that arguing would no longer be an option. They approached their Problem A by addressing their Problem B—that is, by engaging in patient, empathetic, and thoughtful conversation with a mutual goal of understanding. Their new conversation went as such:

Tom: What is upsetting about my wanting to talk about your day?
Elam: You do not hear me saying I am tired. The commute is exhausting.
Tom: Is there anything about me that makes you want to retreat?
Elam: It is not you at all! The office is so busy, I cannot hear myself think. Then I face rush hour traffic. By the time I get home, I feel like an empty shell with nothing to give.
Tom: That has got to be an awful feeling. It makes sense that you need downtime.

Elam: But?

Tom: I can't help worrying that this issue keeps coming up between us. I think we need to go deeper and see if we can find a win for both of us. Regarding lifestyle and relationships, for example, what are your goals?

Elam: What do you mean?

Tom: What kind of activities and interests do you want to share with me? When do you feel most "in the zone" with me? What have you always wanted to do with a partner?

Elam: I see what you mean. I like our vacations, bike rides, and when we cook and host together. But I need a couple hours' rest post-workday before starting anything.

Happy and connected couples encounter just as many stubborn problems as unhappy ones. The difference between the two lies in the quality of the engagement between partners. When we can agree with our partner to communicate in a mutually respectful way, we find that we are able to clearly see and address the core issues above, despite how insurmountable they seem in the moment.

Reflection | Day 12: The Stubborn Problem

Points to Remember

A stubborn problem in your relationship can often feel too "big" and confusing to fix, but the solution always starts with a sincere interest in understanding your partner and a willingness to communicate with them in a calm and goal-oriented way.

Questions to Consider

What "core issue" is currently impacting your ability to solve a stubborn problem with your partner? How is your or your partner's communication method possibly impacting your ability to solve the problem?

Action Plan

The "Getting to Know You Better" Game

Tools needed: Four sheets of paper, two for each partner. Two pencils.

Instructions:

Note: Be patient with this game, understanding that it might inspire resistance on either partner's behalf when you or they feel vulnerable or attacked.

1. Each partner titles one sheet "Values" and the other sheet "Ego."
2. Discover your partner's values. Each partner should write the other's answers to the following questions (additional questions may be added):
3. What is the most important thing to you in life?
4. When do you feel happiest?
5. What do you want that money cannot buy?
6. What kind of work would you do even if you weren't being paid?
7. Discover where your partner's ego might be out of balance. Each partner should write the other's answers to the following questions (additional questions may be added):
8. What topics are you most defensive about?
9. What topics do you tend to overreact, often angrily, about?
10. When do you find yourself feeling insecure or jealous?
11. What can you not let go of?
12. Highlight all information you and your partner deem valuable and incorporate this information in your relationship journals.

Day 13

Reducing Stress in Your Relationship

Is this familiar?

You want your home to give you respite and refuge, but lately it is such a burdensome environment of stress that you've found yourself thinking that work, or your Saturday-night poker game, is a welcome relief from *home*. You may have even sat in your driveway wondering if your neighbor's home is happier than your own.

Day 13 discusses the health risks of stress in general, how to reduce stress in our homes and our relationships, and how to address the stressors we can't change.

In many modern societies there is the unfortunate tendency to believe that productivity always equals success. Many of us have become addicted to achievement and lost sight of balance. So focused are we on doing it all that we are at risk of ignoring a decline in our health and well-being. However major or minor, stress affects how we function, reducing our capacity to manage our lives, and it often simultaneously has long-term impacts on our physical health.

According to a January 2024 poll of 3,000 American adults, 47 percent reported that they wish they had assistance from someone else to help them manage their stress.[1] Many of us have been acculturated to believe that our excessive stress is actually "okay," and perhaps even "normal." Meanwhile, we do not weigh the cost of our stress or, due to a sense of limited time and even financial constraints, feel unable to seek help to mitigate it. While stress functions in humans to aid our inclination toward survival, too much of it has the opposite effect.

Stress is linked to numerous emotional and physical disorders, including viral, autoimmune, and neurological disorders. It is hard to think of any disease that stress does not aggravate, any bodily system that it does not influence; nor is it easy to ignore the negative impact stress has on our psychological states. When the body and mind are in a *constant* state of stress, we can only imagine its exponential impact. Yet many of us not only experience chronic stress, but we are doing so while in a relationship. Not only does our stress radiate out and impact our partners, but our partners themselves may very well be dealing with their own out-of-balance stress state. Over time, one of you may begin to feel lonely and unsupported by your partner because you or they no longer have the "bandwidth" to tend to one or the other's needs. No relationship, and no family, can thrive if any or all members allow their stress to be unmanaged.

Stress in the Home

The reality of stress ensures that few couples have perfect homes, but that does not mean that the stress within cannot be productively managed through conscientious communication with your partner. Let's consider the domestic consequences of stress managed versus stress unmanaged.

When we do not put a premium on working with our partners to manage both our own stress and theirs, we see the results in a house:

- Cluttered and in chaos due to an imbalance of responsibilities
- Tense with unaddressed complaints, avoided interactions, and poorly established boundaries
- Rattled by interruption-laden arguments and unresolved fights
- Quiet with withdrawal and isolation
- Uninviting to outsiders

When partners work together to eliminate or at least significantly reduce each other's stresses, we see the results in a house:

- Ruled by a sense of order, consistency, and shared responsibilities
- Filled with the peaceful noise of productively discussed issues and reasonably set and understood boundaries
- Harmonized in the music of negotiation and compromise
- Warmed by positive physical engagement and shared laughter
- Confidently engaged with the guidance of professional counselors

The trouble with stress in the home is that often each partner is unaware of all the stressors that the other is facing, both due to the fact that partners are simply not with one another at all times of the day, and that partners often do not feel inclined to share with the other everything they are going through. Sometimes, we just don't want to "impose" ourselves too much on our significant other.

Let's consider the example of Jack and Penny. At work, Penny is a perfectionist who juggles more than her fair share, unaware that the owners of the small family-run business consider her their ticket to their own work-life balance. At home, Penny avoids talking about the stress she faces at work, not wanting to burden Jack with her suffering; however, her resentment about her work leaks out at home when she snaps at Jack for small infractions, and especially when she feels that Jack is not attending to her needs. All she sees is Jack off doing his own thing, not truly caring about her, when she needs him most. In turn, Jack walks on eggshells, afraid of Penny's overreactions, upset by her treatment of him, but also feeling despair that he doesn't know how to help her.

In this situation, there are two types of unawareness occurring. For one, Jack feels confused by Penny's behavior and unequipped to reduce her stress because he is not completely aware of what Penny is going through each day at work, as she will not share this with him. At the same time, Penny is unaware of the effect she is having on Jack, as she is solely focused on her own stress and seeking understanding from Jack where she has not allowed there to be.

For many couples in this situation who, like Jack and Penny, have not yet learned the healthy keys to communication in a relationship, an additional problem is that the more stress each partner experiences, the less capable they feel to communicate their stress to the other—and so the cycle continues, the problem becomes a stubborn one, and the relationship begins to break down.

If only Penny knew that confiding in Jack about her stress could empower him to not only understand the cause of her emotional state but also open the door for him to help. And if only Jack knew that if he were to calmly express his confusion and hurt at Penny's behavior then Penny would begin to feel heard and seen by him.

As we'll discuss next, part of the key to unlocking these kinds of healthy and productive conversations is not only focusing on the well-being of our partners, but at the same time considering what we ourselves can start doing to mitigate our own stress. In this combination, we will be all the more equipped to work with the person we love to manage each other's stress in true partnership.

Ways to Manage Stress You Can't Eradicate

At the end of the day, we are still faced with the task of doing what we can to manage our own individual stress, doing our part to ensure we are a healthy member of our relationship. But we run the risk of feeling we are up against an impossible task if we set the expectation that we can eliminate all of our stresses. Once we accept that life will always produce various degrees of stress that we cannot remove entirely, we can begin to apply several techniques of self-care that can reduce our stresses to a degree of which not only we notice, but our partners do as well.

There are five self-care strategies we can all follow to ensure our relationships are fortified to withstand stress in all its forms and degrees:
- Be calm and carry on
- Avoid burnout
- Pace yourself

- Change your perception
- Focus on balance

Be Calm and Carry On

When your life had fewer demands, you may have gotten by without having adequately practiced self-care or had sufficient care from your partner, but as your stress accumulates, it's symptoms are showing more in yourself and it's impacts more and more on your partner. Meanwhile, you may be asking yourself, "How? How can I be calm when my fourteen-year-old is out of control? How can I be calm when my husband doesn't help me in the home? How can I get it all *done*?"

The first thing to remember is that being calm exists outside of eliminating these kinds of issues. The purpose of being calm, rather, is to help ourselves first so that we can help others later—in our case, our significant other and, if applicable, our children. When we are calm, we can react to stressful situations in a measured and productive way; we can address problems more quickly and effectively by being able to apply all of the healthy communication habits we've discussed throughout the previous Days. To borrow the airplane analogy, practicing being calm in the face of stress is analogous to ensuring our oxygen mask is securely fastened to our faces. The better we can breathe for ourselves, the healthier we can communicate with our partners, the more successfully we can take care of our relationship.

Positively engaging in self-care is accepting that you cannot "do it all," that you cannot make all your stresses disappear, while understanding any stressor can be mitigated to such a degree that it is no longer all-powerful but manageable.

Avoid Burnout

All couples have unique needs, but all end up sharing the challenge of managing a home together—with or without children. It can often be in the earlier stages of serious relationships—when each partner is younger and working on their careers, or when children have recently come into the mix, or a combination of both—that stresses can be especially compounding. And yet these are the times that a relationship is especially in need of TLC. But often couples suffer from the "boiling the frog" dilemma when they fail to address their stress; they allow the stress to heat and heat around them until one day they find themselves in a pot of boiling water. We've spoken earlier about the importance of understanding and respecting your partner's need for solitude. Often, it is an ignorance or disrespect of your partner's needs in this arena that allows the pot of water to boil over.

As with all problem-solving in relationships, avoiding burnout is a team effort—even if the primary goal is to prevent burnout in yourself. When it comes to carving out your "me time," this requires clearly communicating your needs to your partner; at the same time, we'll remind ourselves that you yourself have the responsibility of understanding your own partner's needs with regards to their own alone time; despite the normal order of personality differences in relationships, most often both partners require *some* modicum of individual alone time, even if at varying frequencies. If you and your partner allow equal time for one another's own rest and relaxation, you will discover that all else follows—that is, that all other problems can be solved with more ease and understanding.

Avoiding burnout through team effort is equally important, naturally, when children are in the mix. In the years when my children were preteens, I'll always remember our neighbors who designated housework as a team task, completed by all four family members between nine and eleven a.m. on Saturday mornings. They were as coordinated as an orchestra playing a symphony. Then, at the stroke of one p.m., they were dressed and headed to a favorite restaurant for lunch. Each evening after dinner, every family member pitched in to clear and wash dishes, and tidy bathrooms and kitchens—and all within twenty minutes. The parents of this family managed to avoid the couple burnout of housework by sharing the load collectively. And yes, you guessed it, we imitated them, not quite as choreographed as they were, but still with some success.

Pace Yourself

In psychotherapist Ernest Rossi's book *The 20-Minute Break*, which is based on more than twenty years of research, he expresses his findings that when humans ignore the physiological cues that the body and mind are tired, it sets the stage for chronic stress, fatigue, and general system overload. Rossi found that if we take a twenty-minute break from our work every two hours, we remain energetic, healthy, and productive throughout the course of the day, sustaining our long-term health in turn. Rossi points out that between three and four p.m., our body and mind can reach a breaking point if we have not treated it with any breaks.[2] It is at this breaking point that we lose control, that we overeat or rely on sugar for energy, or that we begin to communicate with others in unhealthy ways.

This information left me scrolling through my mind to revisit the times when I would break healthy habits, dismiss motivation, and give in to my impulses. Yes, it was exactly when I was tired after a day of "pushing through," and between three and five p.m.!

What is rest? Rest can be any activity that allows your body and your mind to rejuvenate, even if that means engaging in some form of exercise—rest does not necessarily mean physical idleness. The key is to give your mind the opportunity to float and drift without having to be focused on too difficult a task.

What's important to acknowledge is that rest doesn't come to you; you must bring rest to yourself—and the way to do this is through time management. You must *schedule* rest into your day—but that doesn't just mean scheduling in special time for rest; it means time-managing your other obligations well to ensure that the time for yourself to rest will be available. I learned how to time-manage in order to ensure proper rest from my colleague Peter, who is a master at balancing family obligations with work and self care. The key to Peter's success is that he does not allow "gray" areas and overlap in his schedule—that is, he makes sure that he does not say yes to what he doesn't have time for and can't accomplish, nor does he juggle responsibilities, trading one for another and disappointing someone. Although Peter attends his fourteen-year-old son's hockey games and takes his ten-year-old daughter to weekly doctor's appointments, he exercises regularly, cycles weekly and maintains a practice of meditation. Peter never appears rushed, and balances his time wisely.

When thinking about our own time management in a broad way, it may be necessary to consider the concept known as the "8-8-8 Rule," developed by Welsh social reformer Robert Owen. It is his theory that we were intended to sleep, work, and relax for eight hours each.[4] In truth, you may find that the demands of modern life make it difficult to abide by this rule perfectly, but it's still a good reminder to evaluate just how out of balance your sleep, work, and relaxation is. You may be thinking that you have so much to do every day that your life is just different and more complicated than everyone else's—but it's important to remember that most of us today have found ourselves in the same boat. Looking back at Peter and Maria, it seems that their *reprioritizing* their values was the key to helping them find the right balance, even if it was not always perfect.

Change Your Perception

You may have read new research that says embracing stress is more important than reducing it—at least at first. Though on first glance this advice might sound counterintuitive, the research is pointing to observations about how we actually perceive stress. Health psychologist and lecturer Kelly McGonigal argues that we should approach our stress in a more constructive, positive mindset, arguing that "once you appreciate that going through stress makes you better at it, it can be easier to face each new challenge."[3] In other words, we all have "stress muscles" that, if grown stronger, can help us cope with life's obstacles that much more effectively. Growing stronger stress muscles all depends on training our minds to view stress as a helpful tool for building resilience, not a harmful affliction that just keeps getting in our way of living a happy life.

Life simply comes packaged with stress, some you unintentionally create yourself, some that others generate for you, and some that just seems to come out of nowhere. It's unavoidable, which is especially why we must work to manage our response to it by rethinking our relationship to it.

Focus on the Task at Hand

Here is another lesson I learned from Peter. He explained to me that when life became unbalanced for him once, he taught himself to always do one thing at a time. He explained that "Just one thing" was a mantra that kept him and his wife, Maria, sane and focused on the task of the moment. It was too easy to become overwhelmed with the next hour, or the thought of what was coming tomorrow, or even thoughts about what should have been done in the past.

Peter told me that each evening he and Maria fine-tuned the activities around their daughter's appointments and their son's hockey practices; they assigned certain tasks to be completed on the weekend, such as house cleaning and tidying, and also better delegation of tasks relating to making meals. When a crisis interfered with their plans, they worked together to handle it first, keeping individual self-care in a close second position. And to ensure they maintained a connection, they used the settings of hockey practices and medical waiting rooms as opportunities for soulmate conversations, even getting up at these places to walk the stairs or go around the block together. At times, his wife, Maria, surprised him with a deck of cards or an Uno game from the bottom of her purse.

Notice that Peter and Maria's success is due not only to effectively time-managing their lives, but doing so in partnership.

Use Your Network

It is important to remember we are not living our lives alone. Not only do you have someone to share your life with in your partner, but you also have a network of friends and family. Those relationships, when healthy, can help relieve stress. We'll continue to use my friend Peter as an example of this. When Peter's elderly mother entered a new phase of dementia, she became violent, and Peter needed to manage the details of his parents' lives as if they were now children. Peter reached out to his friends and extended family and, without guilt or shame, explained his situation and asked for help. He admitted he felt overwhelmed, telling them, "I can't do this without each one of you." We all pitched in and filled the sheet of tasks he provided, allowing him and Maria to continue to live a reasonably balanced life.

Almost a year later, when Peter's mother passed away, his community of friends all attended an end-of-life celebration, cried, and hugged each other. We had learned about dementia, how to soothe and calm a patient, made friends at the hospice, and hosted a Strawberry Social for other residents. We learned how to comfort Peter's father, we talked healthily about death, and our children baked cookies for everyone. These were experiences we might not otherwise have had—and all because a dear friend found himself overwhelmed with stress and had the courage to reach out.

Agree and Plan

The key to staying motivated and believing that you have the power to reduce you and your partner's stress, and your entire family's as well, if applicable, is to remember that you don't have to be perfect or, in the beginning, even that good at it. Setting this realistic expectation for yourself will help give you the courage to begin forming a plan with your partner.

As discussed, you must first engage in open and honest conversation with your partner about each of your stress with the shared intention of listening, empathizing, and understanding. From there, you can begin forming your plan together by making a short list of stress-reducing habits you'd like to introduce into your relationship. These initial habits should be reasonable in scope and practical to achieve. They could include scheduling just ten minutes every evening to tidy up a room; or twenty minutes every morning to take a brief walk together. Once you and your partner—or your entire family—establish a rhythm with these good habits, you can plan bigger and bigger, such as entirely reorganizing how you normally approach your weekends, or how you meal plan and share cooking duties. Recalling our networks, it's also important to remember that our stress-reducing habits can involve additional people outside of our relationship and family. We can engage in yoga classes, mindfulness groups, host friendly get-togethers, or even just prioritize calling a friend or relative to share our worries and joys.

If you find that even you're short list of stress-reducing habits feels like an overwhelming undertaking, agree with your partner on what seems the most manageable, if not the most immediately important, habit to form, and set an intention to begin practicing it in more and more frequent intervals—perhaps starting on a weekly basis, then an every-other-day basis, and then daily.

I will leave you with a checklist that includes proactive strategies to help anyone reduce stress and ensure that you do not become the slowly stress-boiled frog. Review this checklist with your partner and place a check mark on any strategy you are already practicing. Make a note of what strategies you can both work on to practice more often or begin practicing altogether.

- ☐ Maintain a balanced diet.
- ☐ Exercise regularly.
- ☐ Make time for relaxation.
- ☐ Prioritize restful sleep.
- ☐ Work on time management.
- ☐ Build breaks into your day.
- ☐ Set realistic expectations for yourself.
- ☐ Reframe negative experiences to see the positive in them.
- ☐ Seek the support of friends and family.
- ☐ Have fun and try to laugh.
- ☐ Seek spiritual fulfillment.
- ☐ Moderate your emotions without the use of substances.
- ☐ Moderate your use of electronic devices.
- ☐ Speak up about your needs.

Reflection | Day 13:
Reducing Stress in Your Relationship

Points to Remember
Within any relationship there is both known stress and unknown stress among partners. The only way to mitigate our own stress, or become aware of our partner's stress, is to speak openly about it and work as a team to address it.

Questions to Consider
- What is a stressor in your life that you have tried to ignore until now?
- What is a known stressor on behalf of your partner that you can help them take the first step to mitigate?
- If your partner is a source of stress for you, how can you open up the conversation about it in a healthy and productive way?

Action Plan
Agree with your partner to each individually identify and write down three stressors in your relationship. Compare notes and decide on one stressor you can mitigate together.

The SHARE Principle

Is this familiar?

You remember back to a time when life seemed so easy with your significant other. Conversation flowed freely, you embraced each other's faults with patience and understanding, you opened your souls to one another on any topic under the sun, you felt protected and cared for at all times, and the fun never seemed to end. But now you sense that your relationship has "closed up" in so many ways. What was once so warm and flexible now feels cold and stuck.

Day 14 asks you to pause and reintegrate the fundamentals of a couple's life together that are so important to sustaining a prosperous relationship. We can understand these fundamentals using the acronym SHARE, which stands for:

- Safety
- Honesty
- Acceptance
- Responsibility
- Enjoyment

Safety refers to emotional security; honesty is related to trust; acceptance opens the door to unconditional love; responsibility is the gear that powers commitment; and enjoyment is what allows you and your partner to tackle life with more ease and enjoy its beauty in union.

Overall, SHARE reminds us that each person in a relationship must share the work to share the long-term rewards. From there, each fundamental built into share can be addressed gradually in manageable doses. As you nudge your relationship in a healthy direction using all of the tools you've learned so far in this book, you can gradually integrate SHARE behaviors into you and your partner's daily lives.

Let's now explore each fundamental.

Safety

When partners devote themselves to preserving the "safety" of their significant other, they are telling them, "I will always respect your feelings."

Providing emotional safety for your partner is a vow to not abandon them or give them any reason to believe someone else is more significant to you. In my favourite crime drama, the lead detective often says, "Watch your six," (watch your back) to his partner with a look of warning and a cautious tone. In a relationship nourished by SHARE, neither partner need worry about watching their back for fear of harm or betrayal.

The expectation for secure attachment and emotional safety is hardwired in all of us at birth. Most of us were lucky enough to have established a therapeutic relationship with our caregiver through the continual assurance of their protection; they listened to our needs and gave us kindness, cementing our feeling of safety. And once we have this sense of assurance, know that we're a priority and that our needs and feelings are recognized, we are able to open ourselves to our caregiver. The same construct of mutual connection is at work in any intimate relationship.

The following chart describes what makes itself visible in both emotionally safe and emotionally unsafe relationships and the consequences, respectively.

	Emotionally Safe Relationship	Emotionally Unsafe Relationship
Actions	Affection, appreciation, attention, respect, validation	Avoidance, contempt, criticism, disrespect
What Actions Promote	Communication, intimacy, openness, trust	Defensiveness, distrust, insecurity, self-protection
Benefits and Harms of Actions to Each Partner	Comfortable with being yourself, empowered to achieve personal growth	Feelings of isolation, loneliness, experience of low self-esteem
Behavior that Actions Promote	Comfortable being vulnerable and sharing feelings and thoughts	Uncomfortable speaking up and sharing concerns and needs

Honesty

When partners put a premium on being honest with one another, they're not simply saying, "I will tell you the truth," but also, "I am who I say I am."

Harvard PhD and psychologist Bella DePaulo, author of *Behind the Door of Deceit*, has studied lying in everyday life for more than thirty years. She says about 64 percent of serious lies involve relationship partners, and that the consequence of a lie is the feeling of betrayal.[1] As I read more about dishonesty in my own studies, I started probing my colleagues and clients about the subject, only to discover that people are dishonest when they benefit from it. The reality is that it is easy for you to lie to your partner if you have something to gain, and especially if it gets you out of a tight spot.

The more we lie to our partner, the easier it might become for us, as we might feel we've found a trick to "get away" with things; we might even convince ourselves we're protecting the other in the spirit of, "what they don't know won't hurt them."

Lies slowly eat away at a relationship, even if well-intended. The best chance for long-lasting love is simply to commit to absolute honesty with your partner. While absolute honesty can be uncomfortable and even painful at times, its function is to engender understanding and even to heal; lying only results in damage.

Commit to Absolute Honesty

There are four concrete reasons that we do not commit to absolute honesty in our relationships, all related to the concept of avoidance. To be sure, none of us can say we have never been influenced by at least one of these reasons in any of our relationships. The key is to put on the brakes when we recognize ourselves acting under any of their influences, and then to reflect on why we feel the need to be dishonest with our partner in any given situation.

Being Dishonest to Avoid Conflict

How often have you heard someone say, "I can't stand conflict!"? This statement telegraphs a desire for agreement at any cost, avoiding argument if only for the appearance of harmony. As attractive as that may feel to you at times, a devotion to conflict avoidance means that you have erased your opinions, ideas, preferences, and personhood in general from your relationship. It will not be long before you feel like a placeholder. We must instead form contracts with our partners to be genuine at all costs—to allow one another the freedom of having an equal standing and an equal voice in our relationships.

Dishonesty through Disengagement

The sibling to dishonesty through conflict avoidance is dishonesty through disengagement, in which one partner refuses to do the "work" of voicing problems, sharing their heart, and seeking understanding of the other. Disengagement may begin with full kisses turning to pecks on the cheek, or gaze-sharing *I love yous* turning to distracted *love you toos*, or invitations to conversation replaced with reaching for your smartphone.

Perhaps the main sign of disengagement in your relationship altogether is that conversations with your significant other have become more of a convenient exchange, or even a business transaction, than a caring connection.

Disengagement may in fact naturally follow from conflict avoidance, as one partner feels they have reached a point in their relationship in which to engage with the other is to risk discovering more and more differences and problems between each other. But as the lessons from the prior Days have taught us, we must remember that any degree of problem-solving is only possible through not engagement alone, but an optimistic engagement that says, "We have our issues, but I believe we can make this work."

Being Dishonest to Please

I wore my high school motto on a badge for six years. Yet, I had to learn that *Esse non videri*, "To be, rather than to seem," was more than just a label about authenticity, and that it takes real courage to risk rejection in order to be the "real you." Even the fictional character Polonius in Shakespeare's *Hamlet* makes authenticity a precursor to honesty in a relationship. "This above all," he says, "to thine own self be true, / And it must follow, as the night the day, / Thou canst not then be false to any man."[2]

Since our earliest years, we have been subtly and not so subtly encouraged by parents, teachers, and peer groups to act in accordance with what they value and suppress our own opinions when we suspect they will be countercultural or otherwise unacceptable. We may have resisted at times, but many of us unconsciously suppress our opinions and deprioritize our values when they conflict with the people around us, including our significant others. This results in many of us taking on what is known as the "people-pleasing" personality. When we are people-pleasers in our relationships, we end up feeling like imposters, rarely experiencing the "zone" of creativity and joy—we may find we're living someone else's life and wearing their uncomfortable shoes.

In a way, dishonesty in the service of pleasing your partner is not avoiding conflict with them as much as it is with yourself. If you realize your relationship is suffering due to your people-pleasing inclinations, it will be difficult at first to reclaim your territory as you include your authentic self in the decisions you and your partner make, and also begin resetting your boundaries. But taking a stand for your authentic self could mean no longer feeling ashamed of your imperfections and the differences you share with your partner. And ultimately, a relationship mutually respectful of each partner's authentic self is stronger, like two concrete pillars standing side by side as they face the future together.

Misunderstanding Dishonesty

A woman in my counseling office once complained she was no longer compatible with her husband as he had changed over time. She described the glow of their former, new relationship when he was outgoing and adventurous, a mirror of her own personality. Although she claimed to value the stability, security, and overall dependability he brought to their relationship, she felt betrayed when these features revealed themselves to be part of his regular persona. She believed that he had hidden his true self to win her over. He disagreed, explaining that he had evolved as he did to balance the needs of their home.

These kinds of progressions of personality in one partner can often be confused with dishonesty by the other. Fostering lasting love, however, is accepting that both you and your partner will change over time and responding to each other's evolution with the understanding that no relationship achieves perfect compatibility. Neither of you lied as each of you "warmed up" to embrace your authentic, ever-changing selves, especially as the needs of your relationship changed. You may also discover that all those original personality traits that drew you to your partner in the first place are still within them, but are only now more evenly balanced with the new traits that have emerged.

Acceptance

When partners realize that acceptance is the way forward, they say to one another, "I love you because of the differences that make you unique. I love you regardless of what you can do for me and what you cannot."

I believe acceptance is the most profound expression of genuine, unconditional love, because accepting your significant other is to accept yourself with humility for all your own shortcomings. And yes, acceptance of your significant other must go beyond words and into action. Acceptance is not submission or agreement but an attitude that influences how you think and feel about the one you love; it shows directly in the words you say to them and the way you act toward them.

The pitfalls on the path to acceptance in a relationship are often lying around the problem of unreasonable expectations. When our partners act in ways that contradict our expectations, we can lose sight of the principles of acceptance—and the more expectations we set, the greater our disappointments will be with our partner, and the more difficult it will be to find our way back to the path of acceptance.

You might see yourself in Laurel, a wife who became increasingly unhappy with her husband Joe's personality differences. As long as she could remember, Laurel hoped for a partner who shared her every interest and passion. But Joe had little interest in participating in Laurel's rigorous health regimen, which included regular gym exercise and outdoor hikes—especially in the morning, when Laurel was most energized, but when he preferred to take his time to warm to the day. Laurel ended up developing a "me versus him" mentality, creating a growing distance between the two of them. In our sessions, it was heartbreaking to hear Laurel's complaints and witness Joe's sense of defeat and confusion as he described his fear of having to give up "his few pleasures in life," and that his wife was beginning to see him as a loser.

While it is appropriate to set some expectations for your spouse, Laurel's expectations were so concretely defined that any flexibility toward acceptance of Joe became impossible. Meanwhile, Laurel had not yet formed an understanding that we can accept our partners "as they are" and still make reasonable requests for behavior change where significant problems actually exist.

Laurel eventually was reminded of the qualities she had always shared with Joe, which her expectations-led distraction forced her to forget. She grew to see how her relationship perfectionism was unfair to Joe, who was, after all, genuinely dedicated to his marriage.

Let us be clear: no one should accept abuse, adultery, contempt, or destructive behaviors from one's spouse—and no one should ignore unhappiness that has poured over into the extreme. If a court in Vermont allowed divorce on the grounds of unhappiness in the mid-1800s, we should not argue that it is unjust to expect someone in the modern world to endure a relationship that has outlived any semblance of love, for any reason.[3] But in our relationships, we must always be considering if our expectations are out of balance with the degree of acceptance with which we should be gracing our partners—and which we would hope our partners are gracing ourselves.

Nonacceptance and Relationship Imbalance

A couple's union is founded on an expectation of unconditional love, a mutual understanding that you are both okay just the way you are. When one partner believes that they cannot be themselves, their relationship to their partner turns into a transaction of pleasing and fitting in, as they become unable to be truly open and vulnerable. In this scenario the very soul of the relationship is impaired.

Dr. John Thoburn, a licensed psychologist and marriage and family therapist in the state of Washington, says that without full acceptance, couples tolerate, retaliate, manipulate, and negotiate with an eye to winning. Acceptance, he says, is not a contractual arrangement between partners who say, "I'll love you *if* you love me." Rather, it is a commitment founded on trust that liberates each partner to love one another despite their limitations. With this foundation, couples have "a platform from which a partner can choose to make changes for the sake of the other, not because he or she has to, but because she or he wants to."[4]

We've discussed the reality that at the beginning of a romance, the differences between ourselves and our partner are intriguing, and we are eager to accept and celebrate them. The more familiar we become with our partners over time, however, the more prone we are to want to "mold" them into an ideal informed by how we understand our own selves. When we do this, we forget that the differences we have with our partners only enrich our relationship in the long run by not only cherishing our partners for the unique individuals they are, but providing a rich and dynamic balance to our relationship as well. One person's frugality, drive, and introversion balances the other's adventurousness, carefree nature, and extroversion. Embracing this balance in combination with a mutual dedication to listening, asking questions, and making *reasonable* behavior change requests ensures that continual growth is made possible not only on the individual level, but on the partnership level too.

The Three Levels of Acceptance

Acceptance must be embraced on three levels; if one level is not adhered to, the others might fall, like dominoes. When the standards of each level are adhered to successfully, each partner feels that their uniqueness is cherished, that their viewpoints are respected, and that they are trusted to engage in problem-solving in good faith.

The following table defines each of the three levels of acceptance and evaluates the qualities of full, partial, and nonacceptance in a relationship.

Levels of Acceptance	Qualities of Full Acceptance	Qualities of Conditional Acceptance	Qualities of Nonacceptance
Partners accept each other's personality traits.	Partners are not in competition, but rather seek win-win results that produce equality.	Partners tolerate each other's traits as long as they determine them acceptable on their own standards and serve their own needs.	Partners express contempt and judgment for differing traits in a self-righteous manner. The relationship becomes defined by fragility and distance.
Partners can disagree without excessive disappointment, judgment, or unreasonable expectations.	Partners listen and ask questions with a goal of fully understanding each other's needs.	Partners hold unreasonable expectations and retaliate when they feel threatened by a differing perspective.	Partners criticize, attack, and avoid responsibility. Fights remain unresolved, problems become stubborn ones, and chaos rules.
Partners do not try to manipulate each other.	Partners promote a trusting and secure commitment, making requests instead of demands, and honestly expressing feelings and concerns.	Partners try to manipulate one another for personal gain, or to coax results from unreasonable expectations.	One or the other partner might feel pressured to compromise out of guilt, shame, or a desire to withdraw. Resentment ensues.

Responsibility

When partners put a premium on responsibility, they are not only showing respect for their relationship as a whole but for their individual selves as well.

There are two ways to think about responsibility in a relationship: being responsible to someone else, and being responsible for what you yourself say and do.

When you are responsible to your partner, you do not just love them, but you tell them "I will" by loving them *in action*. When you do not love your partner in action, they may end up feeling that they cannot depend on you, that you provide more excuses than efforts, that you are not there for them when they truly need you.

The main sign that either you or your partner are not committing to responsibility in your relationship is you or the other continually shifting blame. Blame makes itself known in statements like, "It's not my fault. If you hadn't done that, I would not have yelled." Responsibility can be heard in humble expressions like, "I did not need to yell. I could have said what I needed to without raising my voice."

Committing to responsibility is the antidote to committing to blame. Whereas blame concerns itself with who is at fault, responsibility levels the playing field. Blame encourages all of the unhealthy communication behaviors we have analyzed thus far: making unreasonable requests for personality change, responding to conflict with anger and criticism, aiming to hurt in order to force withdrawal, and generally denying opportunities to problem-solve in partnership in order to protect the ego.

Taking responsibility for our partners and for our actions, however, encourages us to partake in all the healthy communication behaviors a relationship enjoys: accepting one's own role in a conflict motivates us to ensure that we approach problem-solving calmly, patiently, and empathetically; and guides us to highlight behavior in a compassionate way and make reasonable requests for behavior change.

Let's consider how blame and responsibility drive our behavior differently and the overarching results of each.

How Blame Guides Us	How Responsibility Guides Us
Makes us focus on who is at fault	Helps us focus on how we have contributed to the problem at hand
Motivates us to change the other person	Reminds us that the other person is not at fault for who they are
Inspires irrational thinking that leads to anger and the impulse to criticize	Gives us the strength to remain calm and respectful in the heat of conflict
Aims to hurt and forces withdrawal in the other	Empowers us to compassionately pinpoint behavior in the other and problem solve in partnership
Causes us to reinforce negativity and delays problem-solving	Provides a safe space in which to problem solve

In the aforementioned book *The 7 Habits of Highly Effective People*, Stephen Covey says, "Look at the word 'response-ability'—the ability to choose your response. Highly proactive people recognize that response-ability. They do not blame circumstances, conditions, or conditioning for their behavior."[5] In a couple's disagreement, the person who can take responsibility and own up to their part of the problem is the one who leads the way, averts a crisis, and promotes a model for healthy interactions. While taking responsibility does not ensure that the other person will accept their part or make reasonable behavior changes when requested, it still allows you to model adaptive behavior and reduce personal stress—both results that in themselves might positively impact the other person.

Enjoyment

When partners remember that enjoyment is the ultimate goal in their relationship, they ensure that they are constantly reminded that they are friends on a long journey through life.

If you went shopping for a dream relationship, you would undeniably walk past the aisle that said boring, dull, drab, and stale and make a leap, rather, for the bins titled fun, adventure, laughter, and silliness. You may make a brief stop to pick up some wise decisions, thoughtful budgeting, and productivity, but only with the sense that none of these things would be bringing real energy and excitement to your relationship.

What was it about the beginning of your relationship that made it so attractive? What was it about your partner that made you want to spend time with them? I will guess that a shared sense of freedom, of being unrestrained by time, and of being fascinated by your partner's unique qualities had a lot to do with it—and certainly you planned to keep that excitement and spark going forever. But then the demands of life set in—the long work hours, the daily commutes, the meetings, the needs of your children, the household chores—and suddenly you realize that the time for "play" seems to have disappeared entirely.

The truth is that there is always time for sharing in the joy of "play" with your partner, even when it seems there's no space for it left in your lives. What's crucial to remember is that it is play that helps couples maintain their friendship and commitment to their relationship in the long term. When we have fun together, we are able to "mute" the busyness of life and remember that we are always capable of bringing each other joy.

As you've reached Day 14, it should be no surprise to you that the first step to ensuring everlasting enjoyment in your relationship is engaging in communication. If you find yourself in a relationship stagnating due to a lack of joy, you must invite your partner to explore with you what barriers are preventing you from play. From there, you can work together to problem-solve, whether through working on time management, reconsidering your priorities, or coming to a compromise over other issues "getting in the way." It will then be time to explore what "fun" means to both of you at this stage in your relationship. You may surprise one another with your answers—only natural, since we are, as we've discussed, ever-changing as we grow into our relationships.

Consider the following exercises to help you and your partner rediscover ways to bring joy back into your relationship and empower yourselves to make it happen.

1. Separately, write lists of fun activities, prioritizing them from 1 to 10, with 1 being the highest priority. Try to remember what you both enjoyed when you first started dating, and consider whether you might still enjoy them. Don't hesitate to consider what other couples whom you are friends with enjoy doing themselves. Then, share your list with your partner and agree on at least two activities you would both enjoy together. (You can continue to agree on more and more activities as you successfully plan and achieve them.) Decide together on where to place these activities on your calendar.

2. Keep your calendar out and set aside pockets of time where you and your partner have nothing to do. Name these time pockets with general activities that embody togetherness, even if silly or simple, like "Hug it out," or "Laugh a lot." You may both be surprised at how these moments blossom into activities and emotions you couldn't predict.

3. Budget for fun. It remains true that the way we spend our money dictates the color of our lives. Work with your partner to agree on an amount of nonnegotiable money to set aside on a monthly basis that is dedicated to a fun, shared activity.

4. Promote joy by helping one another stay healthy. The healthier we feel, the more energy and motivation we have to enjoy life— it's that simple. Work together to help each other make healthy decisions for diet and exercise. Consider even including healthy activities in your list of joyful ones, whether that is taking bike

rides or leisurely strolls, working in your garden, teaming up on vigorous household projects, or finding a sport you both enjoy.

5. Spice up ordinary moments by adding a twist. Think of ways to "change up" dinner together some nights, perhaps by setting up a small table outside and decorating it with flowers and a candle, like in a restaurant. Or, if you both enjoy reading, choose a book together you are both interested in, and then create a cozy atmosphere in your house and plan "read-along" nights where you read the book out loud to one another. Spicing it up can be simpler and even more spontaneous: if you are cleaning together, put on your favorite music and sing along in chorus as you work. The options for mixing up ordinary activities are limitless—you just need to discover them with your partner.

Reflection | Day 14: The SHARE Principle

Points to Remember

Think of your relationship as a bank account. Each positive interaction is a deposit, and negativity is a withdrawal. Utilize the SHARE principle to make deposits that enrich your account and cushion the occasional backstep.

Questions to Consider

What parts of SHARE in your relationship are stronger, and what parts are weaker? What are the first steps you can take to address the weaker parts? How often do you and your partner "check in" on SHARE, and can you set an intention with them to check in more often?

Action Plan

Create a Commitment Contract with your partner and make it an ongoing pact. On a piece of paper or another platform, write each letter of the SHARE acronym one below the other. Then, agree with your partner on a declarative statement that represents each concept as represented by the acronym, and write out this statement beside the respective letter. See the example below:

S: I care about your feelings and will not be critical, show contempt, or withdraw from you.

H: I will practice honesty, and I will be trustworthy even when it's not convenient.

A: I will accept you as you are perfect just the way you are.

R: I will own up when I have made a mistake.

E: I promise to make enjoyment a priority in our relationship.

The Unconscious Agenda

Is this familiar?

You hoped your relationship would bring mutual satisfaction and happiness to your life, but you're now asking yourself, "Why do I get so upset, hurt, and angry? The slightest thing is a trigger. I do not understand him. I cannot please anyone."

Day 15 will help you understand and repair the hidden drives and impulses that impact your behavior with your partner without you even knowing it.

When the same incident between you and your partner triggers you again and again, and you cannot seem to respond rationally or control your emotions, you may not have the insight to understand how to break the cycle, and you risk believing that your relationship was a mistake. Your significant other, meanwhile, may be confused; they have tried to reassure you and to explain their perspective, and may have even made some behavioral changes but to no avail.

When we find ourselves responding impulsively to our partners in ways and for reasons we don't understand, it is often because our minds are acting on unconscious needs and desires—both of which are often "programmed" in us in our childhoods, and by significant emotional wounds we have suffered. The good news is that we are not helpless to understand this programming and begin to reverse it.

A Word about the Unconscious

Sigmund Freud, best known for his theory of the unconscious mind, suggested that we picture the unconscious (irrational) and conscious (rational) mind like an iceberg where the vast unconscious is underwater and invisible. In contrast, the conscious mind presents as the majestic tip of the iceberg in clear view.[1] Freud's concept suggests that more often than not our behavior is guided by the unconscious mind, which has sculpted for us a way of seeing the world and a way of responding to it that we cannot fully understand. We can keep this in mind when reflecting on the limits of our understanding in terms of why we behave the way we do with our partners. Freud's concept can also remind us that we even *chose* our partners guided by some of this unconscious programming—it wasn't their visual appearance or their personality traits or their interests as much as how we unconsciously *responded* to such things about them. The challenge here is that meeting the needs and desires of your unconscious, irrational mind, especially in the context of a relationship, can be an impossible task.

It is beneficial to understand your unconscious mind's influence because it will often have the last word, the final say, in your decisions. To better understand this influence, we need to investigate how children are raised, and how their early life experiences profoundly impact their unconscious motivations.

Childhood Matters

Even though we are primarily focused on romantic relationships, it's important for us to take some space to explore the ways we can ensure that children are raised so that their future relationships are not overruled by unhealthy unconscious motivations. What this means is providing care to our children in such a way that they grow into secure and capable individuals equipped with all the tools they need to recognize unhealthy partnerships and also navigate worthy, long-term relationships.

We love our children, but it takes more than words—even "I love you" and "You are so special"—to instill a child with healthy "hardware." It takes proper nurture. It is proper nurture that cultivates healthy attachment and helps a child grow into an adult who is capable of intimacy, and who is capable of having the difficult conversations that, as we've discussed, are so crucial to ensuring lasting love.

Nurture and Attachment Theory

The psychological theory of "attachment" was developed in the late 1950s by British psychoanalyst John Bowlby, who spent time analyzing the behavior of infants when they separated from their parents. He discovered that the psychological connectedness between a child and caregiver in their early years had a tremendous impact on a child's long-term development.[2] Later studies by others would continue to affirm that children provided sufficient nurturing by responsive parents were more likely to engage in healthy relationships later in their lives.

We are a bundle of desperate needs as a baby, ready to entrust ourselves to our caregivers for their love and security, but when the signals we get back from them are regularly confusing or frightening—when we experience a sense of detachment from them—we may grow up without the tools to recognize true nurturing behavior. We are then equally likely to be programmed to react in fear and insecurity when engaging with our partners—partners we might have chosen, even, in response to our confusing and ill-directed unconscious impulses.

Known for their development of Adult Attachment Theory, researchers Cindy Hazan and Phillip Shaver explored Bowlby's theory of attachment in the context of romantic relationships in adulthood. They discovered that relationships between caregivers and children and between adult romantic partners shared similar features:

- Both feel safe when the other is nearby and responsive.
- Both have intimate physical contact.

- Both feel insecure when the other is not accessible.
- Both share discoveries with each other.
- Both touch and play with each other's faces and are mutually fascinated and preoccupied with each other.
- Both use "baby talk."[3]

An additional well-known study that makes the case for the importance of early nurture and connection with a caregiver was completed by psychologist Harry Harlow in the mid-sixties. In his experiments, Harlow observed rhesus monkeys when deprived of the presence of their mothers, resulting in the child monkeys having trouble socializing with their in-group later on.[4]

The fact is that parenting reaches far beyond the cradle. The child who doesn't experience proper, sufficient nurture will likely grow to be distant and insensitive in relationships, always having trouble establishing the kind of intimacy with a partner that they actually deeply desire.

Nurture and Ego Strength

Receiving sufficient nurture as a child not only helps to ensure we form a healthy attachment bond that serves us in future romantic relationships, but it also supports the development of our "ego strength," explored by famous child psychoanalyst Erik Erickson. When a child is consistently nurtured, they are that much more equipped to cope with challenges and adversity as they reach various developmental stages—this is the hallmark of having built ego strength. In other words, having built sufficient ego strength is to have resilience and flexibility in the face of obstacles. Erickson claimed there were multiple distinct ego strengths, including fidelity, love, care, and wisdom.[5] It is no wonder that when a child is set up for success with proper nurture in the earlier stages of their lives, they are more likely to experience healthy, long-term romantic relationships; whereas if their developmental needs are not met, what may follow in future relationships is chronic mistrust and an inability to communicate needs and desires effectively—all a result of deep-seated insecurity.

Relationships are Complicated

Keeping the criticality of nurture in mind, we can confidently say that much of our frustration in adult relationships connects to early childhood experiences. If your parents were excessively critical, you may be especially sensitive to criticism as an adult. If your parents were neglectful of your needs, you may overreact when encountering lesser forms of neglect, including unintentional neglect on behalf of another, in adult relationships.

What makes romantic relationships so complicated is that it is in them that we seek to resolve our buried issues and satisfy our long-standing, unmet needs.

We are complex beings with an "old" brain—full of "files" created in our infancy and childhood—that guides our unconscious behavior. When we enter a romantic relationship, the files open, and we feel excited with a sense that we can achieve wholeness through this special someone. We envision for ourselves a sort of ideal condition in which we are nurtured and protected in the way we truly need. We unconsciously hope this "One" will allow us to retrace our childhood traumas, resolve them, and heal.

What many of us cannot understand is that the road to this type of inner discovery and healing in a romantic relationship eventually requires a degree of conflict. The key is taking advantage of conflict to cultivate healthy conversations with our partners that help us discover our unconscious agendas, foster empathic responses, and lead to shared problem-solving.

When Partners Make Their Unconscious Agenda Conscious

Let's consider the example of Anna and Brad, who helped one another reveal their unconscious agendas through constructive conversations.

Anna's father was a capable and confident man and made all the decisions in their home during her childhood. The trouble was, neither Anna nor her siblings were allowed to voice an opinion, and her mother was obliged to agree with her husband. As a consequence, Anna developed a longing for her father's positive attention in her childhood and adolescence, but she was also unconsciously frustrated at her lack of agency as an individual. When she met Brad, she was attracted to his confidence and dependability, an otherwise positive trait of her father's. However, when they disagreed and Brad insisted on his point of view, sometimes interrupting her, Anna's response was excessive: she withdrew, disconnected, and made plans to exit the relationship when it was convenient.

These conflicts continued, and some years went by before Anna and Brad entered my counseling office. I encouraged Anna to describe her years growing up, and gradually she found a way to explain her experience of having felt like her autonomy and her voice had been stripped from her.

Brad thanked Anna for sharing her story, and with further discussion Brad promised he would change his behavior from being authoritative to being inclusive of Anna's opinions and willing to come to decisions in consensus.

A few days later, Brad shared the insecurity he experienced in his own childhood due to his family's unpaid bills, a constantly empty fridge, and other factors of home instability caused by his parent's poor decisions. He described how that deep feeling of insecurity emerged when Anna was indecisive or offering input into decisions he felt was unreasonable or impractical.

Although generally aware of Brad's background, Anna had not made the connection between his disorganized upbringing and his powerful need for structure. She thanked him for his vulnerability, and the couple moved forward with greater compassion and connection, both now understanding just how much open and empathetic communication can allow them to continue to get to know one another on a deeper and deeper level.

Some people are very self-aware and understand how their upbringing affects their current adult relationships. But many people aren't that lucky, or don't have the resources to engage in a professional conversation.

Practice the following exercises to help you explore and discover how you were conditioned in your developmental years, and how you can mitigate the effects of the conditioning's programming. You may find that one exercise versus the others is most effective for you; if so, feel free to practice that one. You may also substitute the name of your caregiver if the words Mom and Dad or "parents" do not apply.

These exercises are done separately and communicated to your partner with a goal to understand each other better.

Exercise: Self-Discovery through Journaling

Assessing your unconscious agenda and addressing your unmet needs can often be done through journaling. Focusing on the targeted questions in each exercise will give your journaling process a useful structure and productive direction. I advise addressing your journal entry's three questions over a seven-day period in a sequential process of relaxation, writing, reflection (learning), and communication.

Relaxation phase: Take five to ten slow, deep breaths, or engage in progressive muscle relaxation by tightening and relaxing your muscle groups, one at a time.

Writing phase: Copy the exercise's three core questions at the top of three separate journal pages. Read and consider each question and try to answer each without overthinking or screening your thoughts.

Learning phase: Using the information from your answers, complete the sentences below each question as confidently as you can.

Communication phase: Share your discoveries with your partner.

You are provided three separate ways to engage with the three core questions—that is, three different "Approaches." You may decide you are only interested in a specific Approach, or you might decide to engage with multiple ones—it is up to you and your comfort level.

Each different Approach to the three core questions prompts you to engage with the questions in a different state of mind so as to inspire multiple perspectives.

Whether you choose to only take one or multiple Approaches, you are encouraged to address the three core questions multiple times over the seven-day period with a goal of making more and more discoveries.

These Approaches and states of mind should be structured as follows:

Approach 1: Simple Mind Preparation

Complete the breathing or muscle-relaxation preparation. Then read, reflect upon, and journal about each core question.

Approach 2: Meditative Self-Prep

Note: Guidance on simple breathing meditation can be easily found on the internet, especially on YouTube. You can simply search "10-minute meditation" to find many results.

Before engaging in the journal exercise, dedicate ten minutes to meditative breathing and concentration. Place yourself in a comfortable sitting position or lying flat on the floor. Set a timer for ten minutes, and begin taking slow, deep breaths, with your only concern focusing on the inhale and the exhale. Gradually close your eyes, and maintain your focus on your breathing and relaxing your entire body.

Approach 3: Experiential Self-Regression

In this approach you will engage in meditation with a goal of reframing your perception of your childhood caregivers. Follow this progression to help you transport your mind:

First, engage in the simple breathing and/or muscle relaxation exercise; or, you may prompt Approach 3 with another 10-minute meditation.

Then, concentrate your mind on returning to your childhood home. If you had moved between homes as a child, you can focus on the childhood home you spent the most time in, or that made the most lasting impression on your memory.

Your next step is to "visit" each caregiver in your childhood home—but first a word of caution:

Some of us, of course, grew up with caregivers who were abusive, hurting us either physically or with their words, or even both. If you suffered by your caregivers in this way, it is important that before you visit them in your memory that you envision them as a healed and loving person. You are *not* visiting your caregivers as they were, but as they should have been. Know that when you do visit them in your memory, you are at no risk of being hurt or punished, and that for the purposes of this exercise they are merely a construct of your mind.

Once you have developed this safe image of the caregivers you will visit, it is now time to find them and engage with them one at a time. Imagine that your caregiver is in a familiar room doing a familiar activity and as you approach they greet you with a safe, warm, and welcoming smile, accepting you fully for who you are and whatever you say.

You are now free to explain to each caregiver what you needed from them growing up, and what they didn't provide you. When you tell them these things, imagine each caregiver listening to you patiently, keeping eye contact with you, nodding in understanding and empathy, and finally, apologizing sincerely. Take as long as you need to express yourself to your caregivers, always remembering that you are safe, and that the caregivers in your memory are now there to help you heal.

The 3 Core Questions

Question Number 1: While growing up, when did I feel loved, and when did I feel unloved?

- I felt loved when Mom or Dad . . .
- I felt unloved when Mom or Dad . . .
- Knowing this, it makes sense that I expect . . . and need . . . in my current relationship.
- When I do not get what I need in my current relationship, I feel . . .
- I have trouble coping when . . .

Question Number 2: What were my parents' most positive and hurtful personality traits, and how did they affect me?

- When Mom or Dad showed a positive personality trait by . . . I reacted by . . . knowing they would . . .
- Knowing this tells me that I am likely to react positively when . . .
- When Mom or Dad showed a negative personality trait by . . . I reacted by . . . knowing they would . . .

- Knowing this tells me that I am likely to overreact or feel hurt and angry when . . .

Question Number 3: What did I need or did not get from my parents, and how did this affect me?

- I most needed Mom to . . . When she did not, I . . .
- I most needed Dad to . . . When he did not, I . . .
- Knowing this, it makes sense that I want my partner to . . .
- When my partner does not understand what my needs are, I know I will react by . . .
- I have trouble communicating these needs to my partner because . . .

Communication phase: Concentrate on eliminating the expectation that your partner can meet all of your needs and that you can meet every single one of theirs. Then, share what you have learned about yourself with your partner in these exercises. Set an intention with your partner in this conversation to explore and discover each other's needs and make a reasonable commitment to love and nurture each other when triggered.

Reflection | Day 15: The Unconscious Agenda

Points to Remember
You seek out a romantic partner in which you find both positive and negative traits that you recognize in your former caregivers. You do so guided by an unconscious desire to recreate and heal childhood wounds and satisfy unmet needs.

Questions to Consider:
Now that you and your partner have explored and discovered one another's unconscious agenda and unmet needs, how will you respond in conflicts with one another where you can see that the root issue is this agenda?

Action Plan
Schedule a time to engage in the Day 15 journaling exercise in conjunction with your partner. Allow yourselves to perform the exercises as many times as needed.

Carry a childhood photo of your significant other with you every day. Take time each day to look at the photo in an effort to "stand in their shoes" and build your empathy for them.

Day 16

A Deeper Look at Unmet Needs

Is this familiar?

You were attracted to your partner because you had a sense, both conscious and unconscious, that they would be able to meet your needs. But you keep finding yourself thinking, "They just seem to disappoint me over and over. I can't seem to get what I really *want* from them."

Day 16 gives us guidance on understanding what we can do ourselves to meet our unmet needs in ways that no one else can.

As we've discussed, the wounds we've suffered due to the behavior of our imperfect caregivers remain with us into our adulthood and drive our behaviors. While they may have provided for you in some essential ways, such as ensuring you were fed, clothed, and brought to school, in other ways they could not provide for you, such as in the way they related to you emotionally. Many of us are then drawn to partners whom we sense can "correct" our feeling of incompleteness and return us to a state of wholeness. We have imagined an opposite to our caregivers and have created an ideal image in our heads of what our perfect partner could be. This idea stays dormant in our minds until one day we meet someone who "matches our meter." We feel that we have found "the One," and our early romance is unbelievably exciting and fulfilling. Soon, however, we may be faced with incredible disappointment as we become more and more aware of the flaws of our significant other and have the realization that they cannot "fill in all our gaps." (We'll discuss this stage of disappointment in more depth in Day 17.)

Let's consider the example of Lynne and Troy to explore how the unconscious needs we could not fulfill in childhood continue to influence us as perpetually unmet needs in our intimate adult relationships.

Lynne grew up in a home where her father was undemonstrative and established his authority through silence, ignoring all signals of sadness, fear, and anger in his wife and children, thus denying the family an emotional existence. She was so drawn to Troy because he always welcomed her opinion and was responsive to her emotions, and there was a sense that her unconscious need to partner with someone who provided for her in ways that her father could not was finally met.

Alternately, Troy came from a family where he constantly tried to escape the chaos and unpredictability of his mother's erratic emotional swings by "flying under the radar." He grew to mistrust emotions and even separate from his own, believing that "emotional people" were scary and unreliable. When he met Lynne, however, he was drawn to her even balance of stability and emotionality, and he had a sense that Lynn could meet his need for a partner for whom expressing emotions was a safe and positive experience.

In the early days of Lynne and Troy's relationship, they resolved their personality differences by speaking up quickly, validating each other for doing so, and solving problems together. Troy felt able to show his emotions in Lynne's stable presence, and Lynn was ecstatic at having a partner willing to embrace her own. But after sharing a home for eight months, Troy's discomfort with emotions began to reemerge as Lynne became more and more open with him, and he grew more likely to clown, joke, or tease in highly emotional moments. He would sometimes walk away at the sight of Lynne's tears, or joke or roll his eyes in discomfort when she asked for a hug, before escaping to the garage. Unfortunately, though Lynne was nothing like Troy's mother, Troy began to interpret any emotionality on behalf of Lynne as representing the emotional chaos of his mother.

In turn, Lynne faced great disappointment in her realization that Troy could not represent the perfect opposite of her father, and Troy faced great disappointment that Lynne could not maintain just the right balance of emotionality and stability to ensure he felt safe in the midst of other people's feelings.

With proper counseling and analysis of each other's unconscious unmet needs, a couple like Lynne and Troy can rebuild their mutual trust, readjust their expectations to align with the "real" people behind each other's ideal image, and learn to manage additional disappointments they would be certain to encounter as their relationship develops into the years.

What We Ourselves Can Do About Our Unmet Needs

We have discussed setting reasonable expectations in the context of our partners in terms of their personality traits and in terms of the scope of what we hope they can do for us on an emotional level. Practicing resetting our expectations along these lines helps us to understand that no person on this earth can completely meet all of our emotional needs—especially considering that every other person is seeking the fulfillment of their *own* needs themselves. Realizing this helps us mitigate our disappointment in understanding that we cannot fully rely upon others to meet all of our needs.

So the question remains: What can we do to negotiate our unmet needs *ourselves*?

The ERA Exercise

The ERA exercise can be used as a tool to manage your expectations of your partner and mitigate your disappointment when they don't meet your deeply held or even unconscious needs. It promotes awareness of your own responses, while also helping you to form more rational responses to your partner when they are not able or willing to meet your needs. Ultimately, this exercise empowers you and you alone to address unmet needs at any given time. Use the following steps in any disappointing situation:

1. **Evaluation**. Ask and answer this question: What am I disappointed about? Why do I feel hurt?
   - Example response: *I am disappointed when he doesn't respond to my being hurt—when he doesn't walk over to say "I care."*

2. **Rethinking.** Ask and answer this question: Are there times when my partner *does* show they care about [issue at hand]?
   - Example response: *My partner does show that he cares when he is not worried, stressed, or tired. I remember that when I complained about being tired myself recently, he started prepping dinner for us.*

3. **Awareness.** Ask and answer this question: How has my new awareness about my partner helped me to think about my unmet needs in a healthier way?
   - Example response: *Even though my partner doesn't always show me that he cares in the way I'd prefer, he still shows me that he cares, just in his own way.*

Setting More Reasonable Expectations for Ourselves

We know that adjusting our expectations of our partners is a healthy way to help us accept their limitations, in turn allowing us to shift our perspectives in such a way that we can problem-solve with them in healthier, mutually rewarding ways. But we need to apply the same adjustment of expectations to ourselves as well. That is to say, many of us carry the false hope, even if done so unconsciously, that we can eventually find some way to fulfill our unmet needs completely, like legendary characters searching for the Fountain of Youth. While we all *should* be striving to meet our emotional needs, we also need to accept that, just like our partners, we are imperfect beings who don't need to suffer the weight of impossible expectations of ourselves.

We can learn here from Buddhism, which discourages expectations as a means to lessen our own suffering. Buddhist practitioner and meditation teacher Phillip Moffitt reminds us that expectations are merely the result of a "wanting mind . . . driven by desire, aversion, and anxiety."[1] Western society often teaches us, meanwhile, that to have few, or even no, expectations is to give without getting back, or to forfeit getting ahead in life.

While we should be seeking to meet our emotional and physical needs, and while we should seek partners who want to help us do so, we should also be managing our expectations about how much we ourselves can meet our unmet needs throughout life. One way to do this is to stop thinking of our unmet needs as a row of boxes all waiting to be checked, but rather as little lakes within us that are always fluctuating in volume. Sometimes one lake might have a lower water level than another—and this is okay; the key is that we always do our best to never allow any lake to go completely dry. Meanwhile, we can try to reframe the way we think of our needs as not "unmet," but rather "not completely met, " or "not yet met."

Reparenting with Positive Emotional and Physical Self-Affirmation

In Day 15 we practiced filling in the blanks regarding how we react and respond in our current relationships based on the types and degrees of emotional and physical care we received from our parents. Depending on the depth of our parents' deficits in this area, many of us have been left without the innate ability to self-soothe or identify and manage our emotions, meanwhile expecting our partners to "just know" how to meet these incompletely met needs of ours, easily bridging the gaps our parents left behind. But as we've seen in the example of Lynne and Troy, our partners are coming to us with their own needs and emotional limitations and can never be expected to fill our lakes of needs to the brim. It is with this understanding that we must practice reparenting ourselves.

When we talk of "reparenting," we do so in the context of our inner child who is still calling out to have their needs met. Reparenting work is applied across multiple methods of psychotherapy in a range of complexity, but always with the goal of lovingly taking the hand of the child within us and leading them confidently through the challenging forest of our adulthood. We've discussed our proclivity to criticize our partners and its harmful effects on our relationship, but the goal of reparenting is to redirect the "criticizing parent" within ourselves, teaching the parent within to treat our inner child with compassion and forgiveness.

We have embraced the reality that our partners cannot meet all of our needs, and that we will always have needs fluctuating between various degrees of fulfillment. It is with this realization that we can begin the daily work of reparenting through self-compassion, and thereby managing our expectations for ourselves in a healthy and productive way.

The first step of self-compassion is committing to practicing it everyday, whenever it is warranted. Self-compassion can begin with positive self-talk, or positive affirmations to ourselves. We can keep these affirmations in the quiet of our minds when we are around others. We can also combine interior self-talk with speaking to ourselves out loud, even in the third person—that is, addressing yourself by your name as a kind friend would try to console you; this method has been observed as providing "enough psychological distance to make emotion regulation easier."[2] Additionally, positive self-talk translates well to journal writing, the key being keeping a journal handy so that it is easily accessible at any time you need to write out compassionate affirmations to yourself.

Positive self-talk can be applied to literally any kind of negative emotional state, whether we're upset with ourselves or with others. Speaking or writing compassionately to ourselves allows us to:

- Forgive ourselves for our behavior: "Reta, I understand why you responded in that way; you felt threatened—but go easy on yourself; you're not perfect and you apologized."
- Remind ourselves that not having all the answers is not a fault: "Reta, you're doing the very best you can and just need to have the courage to keep trying."
- Help ourselves reframe the ways we perceive our partner: "Reta, they know that you deserve love and try to give it to you the best way they can; just remember that they are not perfect either."

- Directly ask the adult within us to guide our inner child: "I'm having a difficult time right now; give me some assistance in making this decision—what is the healthy, well-reasoned thing to do?"
- Motivate ourselves by setting courageous intentions: "Reta, today you are going to achieve what you set out to do."

You must also give yourself the freedom to tell yourself directly, "I love you," as awkward as this might feel when you first began practicing positive self-talk. Take a moment to consider how much of our frustration about our not completely met needs is related to our inability to accept ourselves for who we are and what we are capable of at any given moment.

It is worth considering, even, looking at ourselves in the mirror and telling ourselves "I love you" out loud. Most people are uncomfortable at the thought of looking in the mirror for more than a few seconds to check their appearance. Within our mirrors, however, await the possibility for us to rebuild our love for ourselves and teach us to accept ourselves for who we are at any time. In what is called "mirror work," we can continue to practice first- or third-person affirmation when we feel the nagging disappointment of our not completely met needs.

According to the late motivational author Louise Hay, mirror work helps us to not only learn to love ourselves but also to see the world itself as a "safe and loving place." When we speak to ourselves in our mirrors, says Hay, the mirror "reflects back to you the feelings you have about yourself," making you "immediately aware of where you are resisting and where you are open and flowing."[3] In another sense, speaking to ourselves in the mirror engages multiple forms of awareness as it permits us to view ourselves from "outside the box" of our minds. The majority of our negative self-talk, after all, is done on the interior, inside our minds and within our hearts; but when we view our faces in the mirror and talk to ourselves with compassion, we activate the third-person power that allows us to see ourselves as a distinct human outside the confines of our thoughts, which in turn can help us talk to ourselves as if we were a friend who sees us for who we actually are.

We understand that at the root of our unconscious needs is the desire to be taken care of not just in an emotional sense, but in a physical sense as well; so, reparenting ourselves through positive self-affirmation necessarily extends into the realm of how we physically treat ourselves. In other words, while we can reform our self-perceptions by reframing the ways we *think* about ourselves and the world, we can improve our self-perception in equal measure by making daily, deliberate efforts to treat our *bodies* compassionately. We can begin doing this with the simplest gestures, such as hugging ourselves, gently patting the area over our hearts, or comfortingly patting one hand with the other when we feel sad, insecure, or scared—or at any time whatsoever. In such actions we tell our inner child, "I am here for you." We can then start to consider what larger ways we can treat our bodies more compassionately, including making wise food and exercise choices, setting aside recuperative time for meditation; consuming psychologically beneficial media, prioritizing getting in bed at a reasonable hour, and so on.

Moving Away from "the One"

Couples like Lynn and Troy suffer because they've built an ideal vision in their heads in their early romance—even if done so unconsciously—of their partners as "the One" who will finally fulfill all of their needs. When we allow ourselves to expect our partners to achieve this impossible task, we not only inhibit the positive development of our relationship, but we eliminate the power we have to help ourselves and achieve personal growth. Taking responsibility for our relationships in part means that we are taking responsibility for ourselves; we do this by acknowledging the limitations of our partners, striving to understand their behaviors in an insightfully empathetic way, and empowering ourselves to care for the needs of our inner child in all the ways we actually can.

Moving away from "the One" mentality might feel like giving up the promise of a lifelong partner—but in fact it represents the opposite. "The One" is brittle in our hands; in order for it to exist, it must rely completely on a false perception developed in a young, immature—however exciting—stage of our relationship. In the meantime, both you and your partner have continued to develop as individuals and have continued to know one another on deeper and deeper levels, shattering the idealistic images you had formed. When we move away from "the One," we tell our partner, "I see you for the beautiful person you *actually* are, with all your assets and flaws. I know that you will do your best to meet my needs when and however you can, and I am excited to get down to the good work of building a lasting love with you."

Reflection | Day 16: A Deeper Look at Unmet Needs

Points to Remember

We must accept not only that our partners cannot meet all of our needs completely, but that we cannot be expected to meet all of them completely ourselves. We can cope with this truth by setting reasonable expectations for ourselves, while also treating ourselves with compassion.

Questions to Consider

What are the needs that you know your partner will never be able to meet completely? What can you yourself do to help meet those needs?

Action Plan

As you and your partner individually engage in the ERA exercise and positive self-affirmation, use your journals to record discoveries you make along the way. Schedule a time to share your discoveries with each other. This will also be an opportunity for both of you to acknowledge what needs can not always be met by the other, as well as to show appreciation for the needs that each of you do help one another meet.

Working through Relationship Stages

Is this familiar?

You've been longing for your relationship to be and feel like the way it used to be . . . but deep down you know this is like the impossible desire to hold onto the feeling of being a child again. You've found yourself asking, "Where is the romance? Have I fallen out of love? Am I with the right person?"

In Day 17 we will discover how you can preserve the most important aspects of the "honeymoon" stage you once enjoyed with your partner, all the while navigating disappointments with healthy, balanced expectations.

I have met hundreds of couples in marital crises, and few would have predicted their level of hurt, hopelessness, and disconnection. Partners came into their relationships with expectations about each other's personalities, flaws, and powers to meet each other's needs, but gradually realized they were getting something else entirely.

The concept of human life stages has been written about and researched for decades. And yet a romantic relationship itself enacts its own interior life stages—but many of us are not brought to understand this before entering a serious relationship. One of the most difficult life stages of any romantic relationship is the progression from the early, ecstatic, hormone-infused "honeymoon" phase into the calmer, more predictable post-honeymoon phase. During this metamorphosis, partners can often suffer greatly as they experience disappointment and unexpected conflict, both worsened by a mutual desire to resist change, perhaps even somewhat influenced by a Western cultural obsession with the short-term, romantic stage of love.

Franciscan friar and philosopher Richard Rohr has theorized that what undergirds all suffering is a sense that we have lost control over something.[1] This is an apt observation in the context of our long-term romantic relationships, wherein we are forced to share power and eventually must surrender a degree of control in order to maintain harmony and promote growth.

There would simply be fewer relationship casualties if couples understood the normal stages their relationship will undergo, and could thereby "soften the blow" between transitions and be instilled with a sense of understanding that each is an ever-changing person on a journey not only with the other, but with their own selves.

While relationship stages can cause suffering, if navigated with understanding and wisdom, they are a critical component to ensuring lasting love.

We'll explore each relationship stage one by one, defining them, examining their characteristics, and considering how to approach each in a healthy and productive way. The main relationship stages are as follows:
- Romantic love
- Reality check
- Disappointment
- Power struggle
- Choice (separation or intentionality)

Romantic Love: the Honeymoon Stage

In this shortest stage of a long-term committed relationship—statistically ranging from six months to two years[2]—you often find yourself waking up smiling, bounding out of bed, and living each day with a sense of spontaneity and heightened awareness of the world. Romance makes colors more vivid, fragrances intoxicating, and inspires confidence and energy. Saturated in love, you talk with your significant other into the wee hours of the morning, always seeming to be in agreement with each other, and both infatuated with each other's "cute" and "lovable" imperfections. You cannot wait to see them, hear them, and be in their physical presence. You believe that fate has brought you together.

Dr. Helen Fisher, a researcher at the Kinsey Institute and chief scientific officer of Match.com, and an expert on romantic interpersonal interaction, says that romance and lust result from hormones and chemicals produced in the brain. At no other time but the stage of romantic love does anyone feel the intensity and certainty caused by the following brain drugs:

- Testosterone and estrogen: drive lust
- Dopamine and norepinephrine: heighten attraction and create euphoria
- Oxytocin and vasopressin: allow bonding and attachment[3]

During the stage of romantic love, your unconscious brain merges your past and present experiences in such a way to make you sense that you are at a pivotal place in your personal history—a place where you have a chance to finally receive the nurture you always wanted, righting all the previous wrongs of your upbringing. The experience of romance is so compelling, in fact, that sometimes we seek it over and over, resulting in us passing from one partner to another each time the honeymoon stage ends and we are overcome with mourning, convinced that we had found "true love" and lost it forever.

In Helen Fisher's book *Why We Love: The Nature and Chemistry of Romantic Love*, she explains that "romantic love is a need, a craving. We need food. We need water. We need warmth. And the lover feels he/she *needs* the beloved. Plato had it right over two thousand years ago. The God of Love 'lives in a state of need.'"[4]

But it is exactly at this juncture when we must test ourselves against the next relationship stage: the reality check.

Reality Check: Where the Real Relationship Begins

Whether small or large, it is conflict—followed by its sibling, disappointment—that takes the relationship into the reality phase, the phase in which you realize your relationship will never be quite the same again. Suddenly, you have become anxious about the security of your relationship, and meanwhile, your partner's flaws have become "warts" that you cannot seem to overlook. The man you loved for being calm and careful now seems tedious at times; the woman who once excited your passions can feel occasionally "over-the-top."

It is during the reality check stage that you and your partner must reconcile with a set of unignorable facts:

- Your partner cannot satisfy all of your unmet needs.
- Your words can hurt your partner and cause resentment.
- Your relationship cannot proceed without engaging in problem-solving as a team through constructive conversation.

An essential unignorable fact about the reality check stage that partners must realize and embrace is that it is simply painful to endure. Yet, if engaged in a post-mortem for one of our failed relationships during this phase, we might find that the required suffering would have been a crucial step in personal growth for both you and your former partner. You may even be able to pinpoint that one crucial moment during a conflict when the admission of a mistake, a sincere apology, or an empathetic line of questioning could have rebooted the relationship and laid fresh ground for it to discover a newfound resiliency.

What the pain and disappointment of the reality check phase often blinds us to is the truth that what remains deep within our partner is a beautiful soul who has cultivated a dynamic personality built on their upbringing and harnessed in order to cope and adjust to the whims of their life. At this relationship juncture it is equally important for us to remember that our own diverse set of personality traits, which our partner themselves might be having difficulty accepting in their blossoming perception of us, is equally valid.

Disappointment

As you and your partner navigate your differences, you may find yourselves reacting in various ways, including attacking, withdrawing, or disengaging in bouts of denial. Regardless of the response, you must acknowledge that you're simply mourning the loss of that ideal relationship you both consciously and unconsciously envisioned, and suffering the loss's wounds.

During the disappointment phase, most couples retain a desire to reclaim their former closeness and connection but often feel unsure where to begin, fearing having to experience further hurt and loss. This fear can lead to the development of protective barriers that continue to hinder intimacy. In cases of withdrawal, one or both partners may end up leading what amounts to "separate lives," only minimally interacting beyond essential communication.

Alternatively, some couples may respond to their disappointment by engaging in explosive arguments followed by periods of reconciliation in which they ironically find excitement in an intensity reminiscent of the romantic stage. In this scenario, one partner may withdraw while the other pursues, resulting in a pattern of lashing out and withdrawing from both sides.

Whether evading intimacy or behaving in such a way that recreates a sense of the "drama" of earlier days, each of these responses are enemies of lasting love. It remains critical at this stage for both partners to mutually acknowledge their sense of disappointment; doing so creates a level playing field over which productive conversation can set its roots.

Power Struggle: Me versus You

Even if disappointment is voiced equally between partners, what follows is the stage in which each partner fights to maintain control over the other in order to manage their ideal image of them. Without intervention at this stage, each partner's disillusionment may deepen and their intention to "win" at any cost can strengthen, leading to more conflict and possibly retreat.

At the disappointment stage, partners may even begin to doubt whether they love the other person, and whether the other person loves them, and each may begin to fantasize about separation. We might call this period the "winter of confusion."

The reality check and disappointment phase can be especially confusing to a couple as they both might enjoy brief periods of positivity where a sense of hope creeps back in. Adding to the confusion is that each partner at this stage is likely still not fully equipped to truly analyze whether the relationship can succeed in lasting love.

As it is crucial at the disappointment stage to share your feelings of discouragement with your partner, it is equally important at the power struggle stage to begin sincerely listening to your partner in order to understand their needs and expectations and come to an agreement on which are reasonable and unreasonable. Only then can you begin to discover a new promising direction for your relationship.

Choice: Exit or Breakthrough

The critical nature of the power struggle stage is that the longer you remain there, the more likely you or your partner are to "exit" as you grow more and more distant, whether by planning activities with others, escaping through television or social media excessively, staying late at the office, overfocusing on your children, or distracting yourself with hobbies—in other words, "hiding in plain sight" from one another.

Days and months can become years, until someone finally admits, "This isn't working." In this territory, partners may drift into affairs, even addictions, expressing unhealthy "exit patterns" that cause deeper wounds and add to the sense of chaos.

While we hope that we reach this juncture earlier than later in our relationships, it welcomes in the choice stage, where partners must decide that lasting love is on the table, or that their differences are irreconcilable. The sooner we decide to engage in the work of lasting love, the easier it will be to rebuild your relationship.

During the choice stage, you must build rules with your partner to promote each other's safety to be open and vulnerable, to ask questions, and to make suggestions. As we've previously discussed, this setting for such positive conversation is built on the good faith of each partner to work together to problem-solve in a win-win mindset.

The rules are as follows:

- Celebrate your partner's unique traits and abilities.
- Know and respect your partner's boundaries.
- Tell your partner they matter and can be themselves.
- Practice listening empathetically and asking questions with genuine interest.
- Renew a contract to be accessible and responsive to each other.

As with all relationship conflict, early and conscientious communication is essential to ensuring that all of the relationship stages can be traversed with patience, wisdom, and insight. Couples who accomplish ascending each stage become masters of true, long-term bonding, fortified to handle all remaining conflicts and challenges that come their way as they continue to tell one another an authentic love story throughout the rest of their lives together.

Reflection | Day 17:
Working through Relationship Stages

Points to Remember
All relationships experience the five common stages. Each stage following the initial romance will inevitably involve conflict—but conflict is an integral step in resolving the "big issues" so that your bond becomes strong enough to blossom into a true, everlasting love.

Questions to Consider
Understanding that the romantic stage cannot last forever, how will you and your partner prepare for the real work of a long-term relationship? What stage are you currently in, and what might be a first step to addressing the stage in a healthy and productive way?

Action Plan
Plan a weekly check-in with your partner to "scale" the recent quality of your relationship and to work together to make improvements and set a mutual intention to follow through. This check-in can take no longer than twenty or so minutes.

Initiate your check-in by asking one another, "So, how did we do this week? On a scale of 1 to 10, where would you put us?" From there, you can have a conversation about a negative and positive event, evaluate them, and then work together to problem-solve and congratulate one another where it is warranted.

Before your check-in is complete, be sure to agree with your partner on the date and time of your next check-in.

Five Strategies for Sex and Intimacy

Is this familiar?

You have found yourself sad, frustrated, and divided with your partner about the issue of sex. You might find yourself saying, "We don't have sex anymore, we are like roommates," or perhaps you are stuck on the other end, thinking to yourself, "All they want is sex—there's nothing deeper about our relationship."

Day 18 explores the barriers to sex and intimacy and provides achievable solutions.

Regular sex boosts your immune system, improves sleep, reduces stress, lowers the risk of heart attacks and prostate cancer, and even counts as exercise.[1] These known advantages, however, may not serve well as the motivation you need to reinvigorate your sex life with your partner. Instead, it is important to begin by reflecting on the causes for the drop-off in sexual intimacy between you and your partner. Even before bringing the conversation to your partner, you can privately consider such questions as:

- Are our schedules simply overfilled?
- Am I or the other experiencing hurt that is inhibiting closeness?

- Is there currently a strain in the relationship causing anger or resentment?

The answers to these questions can vary from couple to couple and can exhibit varying degrees of complexity. Here are a few that I have encountered in my counseling:
- The conversation is awkward, so it never happens.
- We've failed to solve underlying resentments.
- We've failed to address past trauma and mental health problems.
- I've given up when there is resistance from my partner.
- We've not yet learned how to collaborate on a solution.
- We're in agreement about sex but haven't created a plan for follow-through.

Sometimes, answers involve the circumstances of the world at large. We cannot ignore that the COVID-19 pandemic changed many couples' lives. Some couples had fewer opportunities to be together due to shifting work needs and cautionary behaviors. Other couples crumbled under the strain of time spent with each other while working from home, as well as nonstop parenting, financial strains, job loss, or the grief of losing loved ones.

As difficult as it may be to consider, however, maintaining sexual intimacy in a long-term relationship is critical despite the depth of challenges you and your partner may be encountering. Three sex therapists I spoke with agree that couples frustrated about sex avoid the subject until it is too late. The three most predominant reasons they cited for avoidance included partners being uncomfortable with the topic, partners not wanting to hurt the other person, and partners worrying about the outcome.

Despite how enormous you feel the barriers are to sexual intimacy with your partner, you should know there's always a way back to intimate physical bonding. The answers remain in the realm of conversation, where partners can follow a five-step strategy:
1. Prepare for a conversation.
2. Talk about it.

3. Make an honest assessment.
4. Develop a specific but flexible plan.
5. Focus on the solution.

Prepare for a Conversation

Your conversation about sex and intimacy must consider timing, turf, and tone: when, where, and how you bring up the subject is critical. You may have a favorite place to relax. If not, consider talking when you are out for a leisurely drive, relaxing over coffee, or on a walk together. Be open, curious, and even prepared to close the subject if asked. If you do have to end the conversation, ask your partner to name a better time to continue. Here are some ideas you can adapt to your situation. It is also advised to avoid broaching or engaging in the conversation while in bed or following a failed sexual moment, when you are distracted by other tasks, or when the conversation could seem to come as a total surprise.

When opening the conversation, we must keep sensitivity and empathy in mind. Before jumping right to specifics, consider requesting your partner's approval to address the subject: "Would you be interested in talking about our sex life?" If your partner seems open to the conversation, you can begin to pinpoint issues: "It seems we've grown uncomfortable when we touch each other. Can we think about why?"

As always, the key is to avoid judgment, criticism, and blame.

Talk About It

We often avoid talking about sex because the subject is embarrassing. You may be protecting the other person's feelings, or holding onto a vague fear of being judged, shamed, or made to feel you are at fault. In any case, the feeling stops you from doing the most important thing: talking about what you desire from your partner, and what you want to give them. It also prevents you, of course, from knowing what would please your significant other.

You may find that when you or your partner begin expressing your-selves, there is a sense of relief that your concerns and desires have finally been given space to come to light.

To guide us in the conversation, we can use the "AAA sandwich" formula: Acknowledge, Assert, and Ask.

First, we can acknowledge something positive about our partner, especially in terms of our physical relationship with them: "I love it when you kiss me."

Next, we can assert a fact or feeling to support your acknowledg-ment: "When we were kissing last night, I wanted it to go on forever."

Then, ask your partner to consider attempting a new strategy to help you both rebuild your physical bond: "I wouldn't mind spending more and more time kissing you and seeing where it goes."

Keep in mind that solving an intimacy issue after a single discussion is overly optimistic, however positively that initial discussion goes. Aim to limit your first discussion to twenty minutes, especially if there's any indication that the conversation needs a pause, and do your best to end on a positive note: you can reiterate the acknowledgement you made in the AAA sandwich, or you can just tell your partner that you love them.

Make an Honest Assessment

Once you have laid the grounds for dialogue with your partner, you can begin to more deeply assess what is inhibiting your closeness. It's important to remember that in order for you and your significant other to speak openly, each of you needs to ensure that the conversation feels safe, and that you are willing to pause the conversation if either of you begins to feel uncomfortable. Your significant other also needs to believe that throughout this process you will remain available and responsive, and that your relationship remains secure. If either of you express or feel disconnection, then address that first, revisiting everything you have learned about building a bond.

From there, you can begin to explore the issues at root of your inti-macy problem. This is a vulnerable stage of honest exploration, so you must remember to remain willing to share your thoughts and feelings in order to encourage your partner to do the same. The more open and honest we are, the more discoveries we allow ourselves to make. Your admission that you are often too tired to have sex after a long workday and would rather go to sleep may result in your partner's admission that they feel like they're bothering you when they ask for intimacy and have thus stopped doing so.

If you end up deciding that your issue requires the assistance of a health professional or sex therapist, come to an agreement on how and when to schedule an initial appointment.

Develop a Specific but Flexible Plan

Whether it takes only a single, productive conversation with your partner or multiple, the key to your success in rebuilding your physical bond is follow-through and, especially, patience. This is your time to brainstorm solutions and make a plan together. You can experiment with a single idea, assess its effectiveness, and make changes where agreed necessary.

Some couples place "intimacy" appointments on their calendars; some find ways to reduce their household workload in order to carve out more private time; others take opportunities to enjoy weekend getaways where they feel more inclined to relax and be vulnerable. Essential to engaging in activities such as these is planning them in consensus with your partner, and making sure that the activities are structured around reasonable, achievable goals. Neither should a couple forget that "follow-through" means "following up," and that partners should discuss how successful they feel an activity was in rebuilding their intimate bond.

Focus on the Solution

If you agree with your partner that one of your intimacy-building activities was indeed unsuccessful, you should focus on using it as an opportunity to continue to seek other solutions, while making a conscious effort to avoid feeling discouraged or overfocusing on a negative experience. Even in an unsuccessful attempt to achieve a sexual encounter, you and your partner can think about one positive to highlight, whether that was a moment of laughter together, or a long embrace. And you can *always* remind each other that each of you tried.

Some solutions simply take more time than others in terms of discovering the root cause of a lack of sexual intimacy within a relationship. Let's explore some of the more difficult causes and strategies to rewind their effects.

Chronic Fighting

As we've discussed, those "stubborn problems" that can nag a relationship can often lead to disconnection and withdrawal between partners, naturally resulting in a decrease or total elimination of sexual intimacy. This was the case of Moe and Adrian, who had not had sex for the last six of their twenty years together. They resisted each other's opinions on everything from saving to spending, children's education, personal career choices, and health. Adrian had fallen into the habit of disagreement, contempt, and separate living without noticing how disheartened and devastated Moe was.

Although they were in my office to solve the mystery of their sixteen-year-old's withdrawal and oppositional behavior, they spent most of the hour unleashing fury and blame. Our conversations about family and parenting were soon tabled in favor of a discussion about the couple's relationship.

To solve their family problems meant that the couple needed to model consistent and authentic collaboration in the home. As we explored practical ways to set an example of togetherness and cooperation, Moe and Adrian committed to regular walks and participating in weekly after-dinner activities with their children. The biggest win was solving problems together with standard techniques such as brainstorming, selecting solutions, and testing those solutions before discarding any ideas. The focus on fostering family pride and engagement improved the couple's relationship.

In a later session with the couple, I learned that Moe spent her childhood with a mother who was bullied by her father and learned that the most demanding person "wins." In a family of three girls, she watched an older sister imitate her mother's "pleasing" and her middle sister consistently fail in repeated attempts to please her dad, both driving Moe to cultivate an independent personality. She thought of Adrian as a good catch when they married but never planned to compromise on anything, and that became one of the factors standing in the way of collaboration, collaboration that later led them to regain physical intimacy.

Infidelity

Resentment caused by former betrayal through infidelity is another common barrier to sex and intimacy. This was the case of Althea and Con.

On the advice of her physician, Althea initiated couples counseling to deal with current and long-standing resentments toward her spouse, Con. With their daughters raised and well established and past the practical hardships of their earlier years, Althea was confused that their relationship was on a divergent path, with Con pursuing more and more hobbies outside the home while she overworked.

She recalled with tears an intimate life that predated her discovery of a text message Con typed to his female coworker back when she was buried in kids' homework projects, playdates, and commuting. When I asked how the couple handled the crisis all those years ago, I discovered that Althea, hurt and busy, buried her feelings and carried on while their relationship eroded into a dance of polite missteps.

Con, burdened with regret at hearing this, jumped at the chance to write a complete and sincere apology without excuses and expectations of quick forgiveness. He made a simple request to prove his love and make it up to her. As Con continued to live up to his promise, Althea's resentment and pain began to retreat, thereby relieving Con's guilt and fear of the future. The couple finally found themselves able to recommit and plan the rest of their lives together.

Past Sexual Abuse and Underlying Trauma

Marriage, couples, and family therapist Tarra Bates-Duford explains that intimacy for a survivor of childhood sexual abuse is typically associated with pain and violation, making it unlikely for such a person to trust a romantic partner. Bates-Duford recommends trauma-informed therapy for such a couple.[2]

Childhood sexual abuse continues to divide couples when the victim suffers silently, and for Dave and Brit, it was this failure to address the traumatic incidents of Brit's childhood that resulted in her withdrawal from a sexual life soon after the birth of their only child; Dave even recognized Brit's decreasing willingness to show affection for him in social settings. However, Dave and Brit were from generations uncomfortable with disclosure. In the meantime, Brit's normal, hurtful excuse to Dave for not engaging in intimacy was "I just don't feel like it." It was many years later before Dave was privy to the sexual abuse Brit experienced in her own family.

When Brit's story of being sexually abused by a family member was finally revealed to Dave in a session, the painful story was unexpected for Dave and uncomfortable for both, but it was clear that Brit needed to "unload" in front of a caring witness in order to safely take down her veneer of normalcy. When Brit finally found herself able to tell her story, the puzzle pieces fell into place for Dave, and he finally understood that her rejection was not his inadequacy or her distaste for him. Although Dave was angry and aggrieved over the couple's lost years, the relationship dynamic shifted from bitterness to compassion. Soon the couple found it easier to sleep beside one another, sit together, and engage in pleasant physical contact with one another in social settings.

Other Factors Affecting Intimacy

You may not want to admit that you and your partner's struggles with sex may have started with your smartphones, your gaming, or your use of pornography. Consider whether any of the following factors has made a detrimental impact on physical intimacy between you and your partner.

Smartphones. It can be hard to accept that your smartphone could be a "third" in your bedroom. But yes, this technology offers an outlet to environments outside the relationship, with its door to social media and a range of other entertainments. It might be time to consider if you have grown more interested in the news and your Instagram feed than the details of your partner's day or their thoughts.

Video gaming. Computer-enabled, widely accessible gaming has been around since the 1970s. Since the beginning, computer gaming has promised to be a habit-forming distraction, for many providing a sort of stimulation that a relationship sometimes cannot. Gaming has been considered by some to be a sort of drug with all the elements of addiction. With the help of behavioral scientists, the manufacturers of video games build in features that produce high surges of dopamine and feelings of satisfaction. Every couple should be concerned if one partner or another consistently prioritizes gaming over time and activities together.

Porn Use. Research as recent as 2022 reveals strikingly high engagement of porn among men, especially those in the age range of 30-49 years.[3] Many of such men's female spouses have reported feeling betrayed when they discover their partner's excessive use of porn.[4]

While some spouses are able to maintain a moderate or even light habit of consuming pornography, for many others it has turned into an addiction that has blunted their interest in their own partner as an addictive distraction. Porn use has also been linked to rewiring our brains' reward circuits into a more juvenile state, severely impacting its dopamine production and potentially provoking depression.[5]

Some of the wider challenges with consuming porn excessively is that it focuses on performance and presents unrealistic standards for both men and women who are in long-term relationships.

There are many other reasons why sex in a long-term relationship may severely decrease, but some others that require special attention include chronic fighting, infidelity, and trauma.

Getting Sex Back in Your Life

There is no hard rule about how much sex any couple should have on a weekly, monthly, or yearly basis. All couples are different in terms of their needs and desires. While one couple might engage in less sexual intimacy than another, they may in fact have a closer bond and experience more long-term happiness than the other. The key is achieving a reasonable frequency and avoiding long "droughts" that provoke a feeling of distance and misunderstanding between partners. (We'll continue to review this concept in Day 19.)

We must also remember to start small and set reasonable goals and expectations when working with our partners to increase our sexual intimacy. Begin with calm and empathetic conversation and vigilantly ensure both you and your partner are heard and understood. From there, agree on those small steps, and don't forget that some of these "steps" can be as simply as paying more attention to the moods and words of your partner. If you plan a date night or a short vacation, keep your plans simple and manageable. If you set a shared intention to engage in foreplay, make sure you both approach this with patience. You can even agree with your partner not to rush the act of sex itself, but rather to focus on smaller steps toward stronger and stronger intimacy.

The process of rebuilding your sex life with your partner will simply take the time it needs, and during this process you will only be strengthening your bond. You're working, after all, toward a long-term, lasting love.

Reflection | Day 18:
Five Strategies to Sex and Intimacy

Points to Remember

Sex is beneficial not only for its physiological effects, but because it supports a stronger and more positive connection between partners.

Questions to Consider

What do you think are the main reasons you are having less sex with your partner? Could you be unaware of some of their thoughts, emotions, and needs on the issue of sex? When is the last time you've had a conversation with your partner about your physical intimacy?

Action Plan

Reframe a positive connotation in your mind about physical intimacy with your partner. Close your eyes and return to a memory of affection, intimacy, or sexuality you experienced with your partner, no matter how long ago. Focus on the positive feelings that this memory evokes; allow yourself to smile if inclined.

Now visualize drawing those feelings to the center of your heart and try to hold on to the experience for at least five minutes. Consider sharing your memories with your significant other.

Repeat this exercise at least once a day as you work with your partner to rebuild the physical intimacy in your relationship.

Day 19

Intimacy Is More Than Sex

Is this familiar?

You still have sex with your partner, but you have a nagging sense that the quality of the sex after your honeymoon stage has changed in some way. You feel unsure, even, what sex with your partner should even be like now.

I believe that sex and physical intimacy symbolize a union of the heart, soul, and body. In Day 19, we will delve into the question of what good sex is.

While what constitutes good sex might be different for every person, most will agree that sex must be driven by the positive forces of passion and tenderness. A series of studies conducted at the University of Toronto in in 2017 observed that positive, fond feelings are a necessary component of sexual satisfaction.[1]

Biology also reinforces and supports affection and passion as being essential to a healthy sexual union, as they promote the production of the all-powerful hormones oxytocin, dopamine, and endorphins. While oxytocin inspires a feeling of connection and trust between partners, dopamine evokes emotional pleasure, and endorphins near euphoria.

Considering the bonding powerhouse that sex can be in a relationship, we can only imagine the risk of extended periods of abstinence.

Partners in a romantic relationship expect, even if ultimately more unconsciously than consciously, a total union of heart, soul, and body. In the same way partners desire availability, responsiveness, and commitment of heart and soul, they equally need to experience this in each other's bodies. When there is a barrier to these qualities in one or the other's body, there is a sense that something is off.

If your end goal is for a lifetime of good sex fueled by affection, passion, and a sense of being fully unified with your partner, we must devote ourselves to the following habits:

- Make intimacy a priority.
- Experiment with sensory stimulation.
- Focus on mutual pleasure, not performance.
- Focus on intimacy, not automatic pleasure.
- Practice vulnerability.

Make Intimacy a Priority

A few years ago, I was in the audience at a concert where the performer told an endearing story about intentional intimacy. "We have a standing date every Saturday night, if possible," he said. "That is the day she gets her nails and hair done and buys a new dress. Later, she takes a long bubble bath and puts on my favourite perfume. Saturday night is when I take her to a place where the food is good, and the band plays the songs we love. We both know that this is our night."

Do you get the picture? This man scheduled time with his partner to be intimate and sexual despite a demanding schedule. I learned that he restricted his bookings to keep Saturday nights free, and that she helped build a sense of eagerness and enthusiasm by planning fun activities geared to energize and excite. Essentially, they both had taken steps to ensure they were in the mood to relax and have the energy to enjoy each other.

Experiment with Sensory Stimulation

The five senses are the gateways into the human physical experience; yet, however many senses we have been granted in our lives, we often forget that they are available to us for making our lives more vivid and our intimate encounters more sensually gratifying.

Experimenting with your partner in activating your senses in an intimate setting should be guided by patience, inspired by curiosity, energized by spontaneity, and resulting in joy and pleasure. Consider setting aside time for mindful touching, tasting, and smelling; do not forget that listening to your partner in concentration, as well as looking at them with all your focus, is included in this spectrum.

Focus on Pleasure, Not Performance

Few people are comfortable talking about their negative sexual experiences. Still, I have heard enough "true confessions" to know that sex might be more meaningful if men and women were more "present" and as interested in their partner's pleasure as they are their own. Being habitually not present or, on the other end, too selfish during your intimate encounters can result in your or your partner feeling like sex is just a task in a line of other tasks, or like you or they are a plastic doll built only for the pleasure of the other.

On average, women say men want sex, but women want connection. What may be more accurate is that they both want connection but seek it differently. If you can accept this common difference with your partner and not allow it to become a source of contention, you can begin to bridge the gap distancing you from physical intimacy with your partner. The first step, which should come as no surprise, is healthy conversation. Make time to speak with your partner to explore each other's preferences around intimacy, and seek to find ways to pleasure one another mutually.

Focus on Intimacy, Not Automatic Pleasure

A relationship where sex for one partner or another is merely a means to gain immediate pleasure is in trouble. As physically satisfying as purely physical sex may be for someone, sex absent of real intimacy and connection will only result in disappointment and distance.

Another way in which couples sometimes unproductively approach sex with only the physical experience in mind is when they use it to try to reconnect after a fight. Although exciting and satisfying in the moment, the danger of using sex for reconnection is in getting stuck in this reactionary cycle and neglecting to solve the core issues that are leading to the fights. Another danger to this tactic is that one partner might not feel as "resolved" following a fight than the other, leaving them feeling used or hopeless about the prospect of actually addressing a problem. Otherwise, while sex following fights can certainly be a mutually pleasing experience, we must do so with a sustained interest in working with our partner to problem-solve. Go ahead and reconnect with sex but do solve the issues that lead to disagreements.

Practice Vulnerability

A man told me recently that his wife wants him to be more vulnerable, but he does not know how. Regardless if you are the husband or the wife, if you're being asked to express more vulnerability but feel equally inhibited, here are some suggestions.

Embracing vulnerability simply starts with the person in the mirror, who must accept their flaws. Admitting that you are as imperfect as the next person, and that you need to feel safe to *be* imperfect around the people closest to you, is the first step. Take stock of your imperfections without self-condemnation or self-pity, and remind yourself that being imperfect does not make you a bad person.

It is then necessary for you to be honest with your significant other about what you feel unable to do for them, or do not know how to do for them, and ask for their insight. Magically, you should discover that your partner has always been an ally who is inspired to be on your side and who will work tirelessly to support you.

When expressing your difficulty to be vulnerable, be sure to use "I" statements and do your best to describe your emotions with an aim toward honesty and openness. Be wary of any impulse to say things for the result of looking "good" in the eyes of the other.

Do not defend yourself in an argument or conversation. Instead, own up to the elements of truth in your partner's statements.

Your defenselessness is not weakness, and nowhere is it more indicative of strength than in heartfelt gratitude toward your spouse. Practice and feel gratitude for the small, everyday, overlooked chores. Demonstrate and speak from the heart about them.

Vulnerability is vital if you hope to have a strong connection. However, if it is not second nature, tell your partner and ask for their patience and acceptance while practicing a new level of defenselessness and openness.

Be encouraging and open to vulnerability. When your significant other has the courage to share their "weakness," listen and inquire without dismissing.

Less Sex Is Only a Problem If You Say It Is

A formal definition of a sexless union is one where sexual intimacy occurs less than ten times per year. But before you worry about this, let's consider that having little or no sex does not necessarily indicate the absence of intimacy or the failure of your relationship. You and your partner can decide together what's right for your relationship. If you are both satisfied with the frequency and quality of sex, you don't have a problem.

The question of sexual frequency in your relationship becomes relevant when one partner or the other actively avoids pleasurable physical contact. In these cases partners need to dig deeper to determine the reason for wanting to create distance, applying the guidance discussed in previous Days.

If you and your partner give every indication that you still desire some form of intimacy in your relationship, it's critical to keep in mind that intimacy does not have to start with sex.

Intimacy: More Than Just Sex

As distressed as we might feel about the lack of sexual intimacy that has developed in our relationship, we must remember that physical intimacy can be enjoyed in smaller ways and in smaller steps, and that intimacy itself begins with a sense of togetherness.

Intimacy is founded upon compassionate words and touch, even outside of a sexual context. In a famous study conducted in 1947, researchers René Spitz and Katherine Wolf discovered that infants who do not receive sufficient touch and other forms of attentive human contact may die prematurely.[2] Research today continues to reveal that receiving positive physical touch from another is an extremely effective communicator of compassion, love, and gratitude, and that without it, our mental and physical well-being suffers. This research also observes that a positive impact on well-being is guaranteed by compassionate touch despite the duration and the nature of the touching. "A long-lasting massage by a therapist," it's been observed, "could therefore be just as effective as a quick hug offered by a friend." What *does* matter concerning touch, the research finds, is the frequency with which we experience it.[3]

The Simple Act of Holding Hands

Did you know that the simple act of holding hands releases the feel-good neurotransmitter oxytocin, leading to a shared sense of safety and trust?[4] Sadly, many individuals grew up in homes where hugging, nurturing caresses, or even the supportive pat of recognition was rare, and they learned early to distance themselves physically from others. For such people, bonding in a relationship's courtship period may only mean sexual intercourse, leading to the neglect of other forms of intimate touch.

Western men are especially victims of a culture that has shamed touching and the vulnerability and dependence that it engenders, leaving them in a deficit with the women they love. The most heartbreaking stories I hear in counseling come from couples who separate because of these childhood-originating barriers. The following is a story about a young couple whose sexual life ended because of his discomfort with touch.

Ruth and Adam were compatible, thoughtful, and sensitive to each other, but when the early days of romance ended, Adam sought the far end of the couch, and she noticed that when she reached for his hand, he dropped it soon after. At the end of a day of caring for their five-month-old, Ruth needed her husband's reassurance and affection in the form of simple touch, but as the months wore on and Adam could not provide this degree of physical intimacy, she found herself turning away from his more blatant sexual advances. As a result, Adam felt that Ruth was being selfish and punishing him.

"I feel sexy, desirable, and wanted when you touch me," was Ruth's honest and vulnerable statement to Adam in their counseling appointment. In response, Adam admitted that physical contact was infrequent in his childhood home and it made him feel uncomfortably vulnerable and unsafe. He expressed that Ruth's hand-holding advances and attempts to snuggle felt forced and manipulative.

It was my turn to suggest how the couple could practice touch without a sense of it being demanded or forced by Ruth. This exercise was more fruitful than I could have hoped, and the couple developed a plan for simple touch that, practiced over several months, proved to become second nature. The exercise went as follows:

Ruth was to reach for Adam's hand and caress it, while Adam was to close his eyes, visualizing himself relaxed and smiling in contentment. If Adam needed Ruth to do something different, it was understood that he was allowed to make a request.

Holding with Intention

When we take our time holding one another, whether with our hands or onto each other's bodies, it elevates our experience of intimacy to a new level.

Intimate holding is not momentary grabbing, clutching, or restraining. It is not casual or half-conscious but deliberate and comforting. To hold someone is to express the full range of loving emotions unselfishly and courageously. Without words, holding speaks to the heart in a vibrant language of true unity.

You can hold your partner sitting, standing, or lying down, the key being physical and emotional comfort. When we hold each other intentionally, the result should be time and space fading away, with a feeling that we are simply existing with each other without expectation, simply waiting for the next moment to arrive.

A final goal of holding is to learn to listen to our partners and be able to hear them when say they are ready to release, telling you, "I am filled and overflowing."

Intimacy-Building Exercise

In 1997 Arthur Aron and Elaine Spaulding, researchers at the University of California at Berkeley and a romantic couple, developed a list of thirty-six questions, organized into three sets, which pairs of strangers were to ask one another. Their aim was to discover a way to create instant intimacy between total strangers. Based on their own experience of attraction and marriage, they established that sharing personal and sensitive information while looking into each other's eyes for four minutes would significantly provoke attraction.[5]

In the whirlwind of tasks and obligations in any couple's life following those easy, early days of romance, it is common that deep, intimacy-building conversations between partners can dwindle or become infrequent. Sometimes the problem is that we feel we know our partners so well that access to further deep, interesting, intimate conversation might seem closed off. We should know, however, that the door to intimacy through conversation is always open—sometimes we just need a structure to work off of.

My challenge to you is to work through the thirty-six questions designed by Aron and Spaulding in the mindset of someone who is meeting your partner for the first time. Questions should be engaged one at a time while holding eye contact—and by Day 19 we should all know that we need to listen to our partners as if our lives depended on really *knowing* our partners. Consider envisioning your partner as someone who is completely new to you as you both engage in the thirty-six questions. Below are the three sets of questions reproduced exactly in their original form.

I will introduce these questions with a quote to help you reflect on the importance of openness and honesty in ensuring lasting love:

> *"Secrecy is the enemy of intimacy. Every healthy relationship is built on a foundation of honesty and trust."*
> —Relationship Expert Dave Willis

Arthur Aron and Elaine Spaulding's 36 Questions

(These questions are also accessible from various online sources.)

Set I

1. Given the choice of anyone in the world, whom would you want as a dinner guest?
2. Would you like to be famous? In what way?
3. Before making a telephone call, do you ever rehearse what you are going to say? Why?
4. What would constitute a "perfect" day for you?
5. When did you last sing to yourself? To someone else?
6. If you were able to live to the age of 90 and retain either the mind or body of a 30-year-old for the last 60 years of your life, which would you want?
7. Do you have a secret hunch about how you will die?
8. Name three things you and your partner appear to have in common.
9. For what in your life do you feel most grateful?
10. If you could change anything about the way you were raised, what would it be?

11. Take four minutes and tell your partner your life story in as much detail as possible.
12. If you could wake up tomorrow having gained any one quality or ability, what would it be?

Set II
13. If a crystal ball could tell you the truth about yourself, your life, the future or anything else, what would you want to know?
14. Is there something that you've dreamed of doing for a long time? Why haven't you done it?
15. What is the greatest accomplishment of your life?
16. What do you value most in a friendship?
17. What is your most treasured memory?
18. What is your most terrible memory?
19. If you knew that in one year you would die suddenly, would you change anything about the way you are now living? Why?
20. What does friendship mean to you?
21. What roles do love and affection play in your life?
22. Alternate sharing something you consider a positive characteristic of your partner. Share a total of five items.
23. How close and warm is your family? Do you feel your childhood was happier than most other people's?
24. How do you feel about your relationship with your mother?

Set III
25. Make three true "we" statements each. For instance, "We are both in this room feeling . . . "
26. Complete this sentence: "I wish I had someone with whom I could share . . . "
27. If you were going to become a close friend with your partner, please share what would be important for him or her to know.
28. Tell your partner what you like about them; be very honest this time, saying things that you might not say to someone you've just met.

29. Share with your partner an embarrassing moment in your life.

30. When did you last cry in front of another person? By yourself?

31. Tell your partner something that you like about them already.

32. What, if anything, is too serious to be joked about?

33. If you were to die this evening with no opportunity to communicate with anyone, what would you most regret not having told someone? Why haven't you told them yet?

34. Your house, containing everything you own, catches fire. After saving your loved ones and pets, you have time to safely make a final dash to save any one item. What would it be? Why?

35. Of all the people in your family, whose death would you find the most disturbing? Why?

36. Share a personal problem and ask your partner's advice on how he or she might handle it. Also, ask your partner to reflect back to you how you seem to be feeling about the problem you have chosen.

Reflection | Day 19: Intimacy Is More Than Sex

Points to Remember
In the same way we desire a nonphysical connection of heart and soul with our partners, we need physical connection in physical intimacy. We have a sense that something is wrong when we have stopped engaging in touch.

Questions to Consider
Using the guidance of Day 19, what small steps can you take with your partner to gradually incorporate physical intimacy back into your relationship?

Action Plan 1
Guided by the advice in Day 19, write down three things you would like to try with your partner to rebuild intimacy. Remember that sex does not always have to be the goal with intimacy. Share your ideas with your partner and agree on a first strategy to try together.

Day 20

Happiness Is Not Automatic

Is this familiar?

You know something is wrong between you and your partner, but you tell yourself, "If we really love each other, everything will just work out on its own."

Through my years of practice, I've seen many struggling couples held back from real solutions due to one partner or both holding this belief. Consequently, they don't put in the work it takes to have a good relationship. In working through Day 20, you will learn happiness in your relationship is not automatic, but it is worth the effort it takes to get there.

Considering the Western societal isolation caused by variables like social media, upward trends in working from home and in work hours themselves, having to move away from our families, losing contact with our childhood friends, and even the divisiveness of politics, romantic relationships in the twenty-first century are more important than ever. They fill the gap that isolation from neighbours and families have created. As early as 1916, L. J. Hanifan, a Virginia educator, documented a connection between what he termed "social capital"—the wealth gained from the experience of fellowship and mutual sympathy between people in a society—and overall individual well-being and life satisfaction.[1]

We all need long-term, intimate relationships, but many of us have little idea of how to sustain a fulfilling relationship, expecting or hoping for them, rather, to just happen. This unrealistic expectation is prompted in part by fairytales and childhood stories in our culture that promote easy magic and happily-ever-after narratives. *Cinderella*, *Sleeping Beauty*, and *The Little Mermaid*, for example, depict romances where a pursuer climbs mountains and endures hardships to find and win his true love. Fireworks spark and fly, hearts and ribbons flutter all around, expensive rings slide easily onto fingers, and the scenes continue to blossom with dramatic entrances and displays of love and romance on the sunniest June day of the year. Hollywood movies, books, and even music have led us to believe that all a couple needs to ensure lasting happiness is early love.

Where Did the Magic Go?

With the gradual entrance of all of life's realities, romantic relationships rarely play out as "happily ever after" fairytales. Partners experience loss, disappointment, and crisis, as a couple and individually. Stress and exhaustion accumulate, and despite our best intentions, we often find ourselves overwhelmed by routine as we maintain the important yet uninspiring obligations and tasks. With this drain on energy and resources, we often feel as if we've failed to live up to the promises we've made to our partners and to achieve our primary goal: to steadfastly love and nurture each other.

Such struggling couples who lack guidance and mentorship often end up assuming they have come to a definitive end with no hope of remedy, telling one another, "I love you, but I am not in love with you," or "We were just not meant to be." Such couples too often forget that their frustration with their relationships is merely a reaction to the normal ebbs and flows of human life, and that these are the times when true, lasting love is meant to be built.

Couples often just need a fresh start and a good plan with which to rebuild their bond. Especially if you are the one considering taking flight from your relationship, it's important that you pause to honestly ask yourself, "Am I mistakenly seeking something that could be there all along? Can true, lasting love still be in the cards here?"

Diamond in the Rough

Think of your relationship as a diamond in the rough.

A diamond is formed more than ninety miles below the earth's surface and requires backbreaking hours of digging, sifting, and screening through rocks, dirt, and grime to access. From there, there is the cutting and polishing before the stone even warrants inspection. It takes patience to achieve a stone of value.

A healthy relationship requires the same patience. You need the ability to look below the surface and commit to the entire process from start to finish. This kind of work takes perseverance and devotion, and the few who stay in the game reap the rewards of personal growth and lasting love. Only a diamond can cut a diamond, and only in relationships can we be sharpened and prepared to be the best version of ourselves.

Putting in the Work

Through my work with couples, I have come across many who had a great connection at the beginning of their relationship, but over time they failed to achieve lasting love. Karen and Darren are one example.

When Karen met Darren on a blind date that her girlfriend arranged, she was divorced and parenting a five-month-old. Karen and Darren's attraction was instant, but it did not develop into true, lasting love.

When I met the couple, they were two years married with an infant in addition to Karen's now four-year-old child. Their eyes and body language confirmed they were equally confused, miserable, disconnected, and they barely spoke to one another. Darren had developed trust issues with Karen and said he just "didn't feel the way he did before" about the relationship; and Karen was distraught about how Darren had shifted his priorities to spending more time at work and with friends than at home with her. Karen ultimately felt she couldn't handle Darren's silence and anger any longer.

Darren and Karen could not see that they were at a juncture in which they could work together to forge a future built on true love for their relationship, and they were not a consumable package of temporary happiness. When they made the decision to do the work, I guided the couple in taking their next steps toward building truly lasting love. To many couples' surprise, these steps await them exactly when it seems there is no hope remaining for their relationship.

I explained to Darren and Karen how their next steps were founded upon healthy communication and follow-through.

First, I asked the couple to acknowledge their mutual disappointment, as well as their unhealthy relationship patterns, including their withdrawal from one another. They were to next admit that their current relationship patterns were destructive and only perpetuated their disconnection. From there, the couple was to take the next step of practicing daily communication, following these simple rules:

1. Introduce an issue by taking ownership, leading with phrases like "I feel," "I notice," or "I would like."

2. Provide feedback that refrains from any form of attack on the other person, shared with the spirit of empathy and patience, beginning your reply in ways such as "I had no idea you felt this way," or "I still do not understand. Please tell me more."

3. Replace defensive responses, including excuses and "but" replies, with sincere and compassionately formed questions.

4. Remain open and vulnerable about your needs, allowing your significant other to really understand and "see" you; feel free to express yourself with phrases like "I hope we might," and "I'd like to try . . ."

5. Hold weekly "town halls" ranging from twenty to thirty minutes with a goal of addressing issues logically and in partnership as

they arise, all the while abiding by the rules of healthy conversation collected across all of the Days so far.

6. Rebuild trust by applying an agreed upon, respectful way to signal to each other when a communication adjustment is needed, such as raising a small yellow flag to indicate a request for a rephrase.

After several weeks of practicing healthy communication and "town halls," Karen expressed that "Our conversations are drawing us closer," and I agreed, seeing it with my own eyes.

No, relationship happiness is not automatic—it takes work to create true, lasting love.

Finding Balance and Gratitude

In a healthy and lasting relationship, we should not only communicate to understand one another, effectively pinpoint issues, and problem solve together, but to continually find balance by acknowledging *why* we love the other and why our lives would be less fulfilled without them. The story of Kevin and Stephanie illustrates how it's important to find balance through gratitude in a relationship.

In an age when so many people meet online, Kevin and Stephanie believed it was fate that drew them instead to the same hotel thousands of miles away from home, even though they grew up and lived in the same city. On vacation, they saw each other daily and enjoyed diving, museums, and long walks. What are the chances?

Yet here they were in my office. In less than two years they faced a fizzling romance, suffering from exhaustion and confusion about what went wrong.

As an emergency doctor, Kevin assumed that Stephanie would understand his long, irregular hours, but after spending evenings and weekends alone, Stephanie soon rekindled an old flame on social media. A few frank conversations revealed the gap between Kevin and Stephanie's relationship expectations, and it was clear that the couple would not get back on the same page without the necessary listening and questioning that would help them redefine their commitment to each other.

Stephanie and Kevin were uncomfortable in a therapist's office. They saw themselves as capable and skilled people who should not have the kinds of problems that needed outside help. But they were here because a friend said they should talk to someone.

I suggested to the couple that separation was always an option, and it was reasonable to expect to meet someone else within a few years. I reminded them, though, that every new person they met would never be perfectly ideal, with their own flaws and deficits.

After putting this in mind against their consideration of separation, I discussed the delicate balance of negotiating the needs of each person with the needs of the relationship, pointing out that relationships need time for each person to grow and positive experiences to enrich them. This could mean Kevin making a commitment to weekly date nights and weekends away and Stephanie making an effort to reconnect with friends, take up hobbies, and get involved in community service.

I asked Kevin and Stephanie to participate in a gratitude exercise that would help them see the rewards of balance in their relationship, and also encourage them to celebrate one another in the spirit of mutual acceptance. On a weekly basis, each partner was to use a "gratitude notebook" to list each other's assets, acknowledge each other's contributions to their relationship, and point out improvements each have made. They were then to share their observations with one another. A couples' gratitude notebook may have entries as simple as the following:

- I am grateful that we laughed together.
- I am glad for our Sunday brunch this week.
- I appreciate that you were available for this exercise.

As the couple continued to make adjustments for one another to bring more balance to their relationship—Stephanie finding more ways to enrich her life as an individual, and Kevin making adjustments to his work schedule to afford him some more personal time with

Stephanie—they grew to find gratitude in even the smallest, random interactions they had with one another, further cultivating a positive relationship mindset suited for long-lasting love.

Couples like Stephanie and Kevin discovered happiness not because they waited for it to arrive at their doorstep, but because they did the necessary work. They learned that relationship happiness is built on a daily basis, and relies on healthy conversations that embraces vulnerability, honesty, empathy, and teamwork. They also accepted that relationship balance is always in flux—one day they might be at 60/40, but if they work together, they can find 50/50 again soon. Finally, Kevin and Stephanie learned that the work that goes into sustaining gratitude and maintaining balance is not always easy, but it continually proves that it is possible.

Reflection | Day 20: Happiness Is Not Automatic

Points to Remember

The excitement of romantic love misleads us into thinking that when it's gone, so is love itself. "True love," however, is that which is built to last—but it takes work and the patience to do so in small, manageable steps.

Questions to Consider

When do you think you began to feel that your relationship started to lose its happy, romantic energy? How much is your degree of disappointment related to your degree of gratitude, or lack thereof? What might you lose by exiting your relationship, and what might you gain by staying and trying to build a stronger love with your partner?

Action Plan

Consider attempting the "next steps" that Darren and Karen found so helpful. If necessary, decide on just one of the steps to take with your partner, and allow yourselves to be patient as you practice it. Make sure that the goals you set are small and manageable.

Day 21

Connection Is the Key

Is this familiar?

When speaking to yourself or your significant other, you say, "We are just going through the motions. We used to be *so close* to one another, but now we've grown apart."

If this rings true to you, you are not alone. In one study of couples suffering relationship breakdowns, nearly two-thirds of participants cited three major reasons for relationship unhappiness, one of the reasons being "growing apart."[1]

In Day 21 we explore how to rediscover and reinstall the core connection we once enjoyed with our partner and learn how to feed and strengthen it so it lasts.

If healthy relationships were pyramids, the element of connection would be the foundational base on top of which all of the other parts are built. You can even imagine connection as the engine of a relationship, effective communication the fuel that powers it.

The connection bond is both an invisible force shared between partners and a visible bond that partners and others can see in action as well. Without real connection, no relationship can weather the elements of time.

Research continues to support the thesis that a deep and loving connection in a long-term relationship not only nurtures our need for security established in our childhood, but is what continually whets our relationship appetite, so to speak, following the early honeymoon stage. In her research for her book *Hold Me Tight*, couples therapist Sue Johnson discovered that "in a secure relationship, excitement comes not from trying to resurrect the novel moments of infatuated passion but from the risk involved in staying open in the moment-to-moment, here-and-now experience of physical and emotional connection."[2] In *Getting the Love You Want*, aforementioned relationship expert Harville Hendrix makes the case that at the core of every fight and disagreement in a relationship is a plea for more connection.[3]

The primary reason couples grow apart is not because of their disagreements per se, but because they've failed to sustain a connection by *working through* their disagreements. Unaddressed disagreements result in hurtful words and actions that create a narrative—even if a false one—that tells the story of people saying to one another, "I am not *available* to you, I won't be *responsive* to you, you don't *matter*."

In my experience working with couples, I've discovered the truth that it is much easier to do the work of preserving a connection than it is to repair a broken one—but that does not mean a broken one cannot be repaired with honest intention and perseverance.

Whether you're in a relationship whose connection is damaged or entirely broken, there are three connection strategies you can use to nurture it back to life and keep it thriving. These strategies include cultivating the Open ARMS attitude, practicing mindful togetherness, and cultivating honest conversation.

Connection Strategy 1: Open ARMS Attitude

The ARMS attitude is built on the concept that in a relationship of lasting love, each partner is each other's number one priority. The signs that a couple has adopted an ARMS attitude are both visible and invisible: visible in the way they make physical contact and communicate through bodily gestures and facial expressions, and invisible in terms of the nonphysical threads of familiarity and trust strung between them. The ARMS attitude cannot be manufactured out of thin air, but rather must, as with all the real work that goes into building lasting love, be formed into a habit with continual, conscious effort. The ARMS acronym embodies a promise, represented in the core elements of lasting connection:

Available: I will be available to you.

Responsive: I will be responsive to you.

Matter: You will always matter most to me.

Stay close: I will stay close to you.

When you lock eyes across a room with your significant other and your gaze communicates admiration and tenderness, and you are able to hold that gaze feeling comfortable in the other's; and when you listen to your partner attentively and seek to understand their needs, feelings, and desires, you have answered the question: Am I available to you?

When you celebrate your partner's unique personality by actively showing interest in their ideas, opinions, hobbies, and talents; and when you show respect for the values they hold that differ from your own, you have answered the question: Am I responsive to you?

When you make personal and family decisions only after ensuring mutual understanding and agreement with your partner; and when you stand up for your partner when they are vulnerable and need support, you have answered the question: Do I show you that you matter most?

And when you prioritize your partner's needs above work, friends, and family; and when you patiently accompany them through their most difficult times in life no matter your own discomfort and pain, you have answered the question: Will I stay close to you?

As with all other guidance from previous Days, developing an ARMS attitude takes daily work and the belief that your relationship is worth rebuilding into a bond of lasting love. We are all human, and no one can always perfectly follow the guidance of ARMS, but it is a habit like any other—the more you try, the stronger the habit becomes.

Connection Strategy 2: Practice Mindful Togetherness

It's easy to fall into the habit of "doing" life instead of living it. We get so wrapped up in the "busyness" of life and all its obligations—whether it's getting the kids ready for school, driving to work, shopping for groceries, making meals, cleaning the house, or mowing the lawn—that even when we get a chance to spend quality time with our significant other, our minds may still be reliving the day at the office, planning the grocery list, or thinking about tomorrow's appointments. We may find ourselves still "doing" together, rather than *being* together, when we finally get the chance to cuddle on the couch, or take a long walk, or cook together, and so on. All the while, deep down we still want and need the deep connection that doesn't live in the past or the future, but only in the present.

Research reveals that attempts at mindfulness practice have seen a significant upswing in Western culture since 2006.[4] This is no surprise to anyone who has found themselves stuck in the "grind" of modern life and seeking a way to slow down their minds, channel their thoughts, and truly exist in the present. But how do two individuals, both overwhelmed with thoughts of yesterday and concerns about tomorrow, adjust their mindsets so that they can truly enjoy the special time they have together?

Regardless of whether you and your partner are engaged in an essential task that falls into the "busyness" routine or sitting down together to play a card game, mindful togetherness is an equally important, however difficult, goal. One strategy you and your partner can use to engage mindful togetherness is simply taking the moment together to *stop*. Think of stopping as employing the healthy relationship habit of empathetic listening. Whether you are both in the middle of a task, or about to begin one, agree with your partner to first stop, share each other's gaze, and breathe calmly with one another. You can also consider letting each other voice the thoughts that are keeping you from being in the present and fully enjoying the presence of your partner. Give your thoughts the freedom to make an exit, then, by each saying out loud, "It's okay to let my thoughts go for right now so that I can enjoy being together with you." In this strategy, we are listening to our own thoughts and the thoughts of our partner, and then we are listening to the needs of our soul and our partner's soul. When you and your partner are ready, you can agree to "start" your task or activity again, whether it was washing dishes or working in your garden. Upon returning, you can both remember to let your senses guide your feeling of connection—that is, being mindful of what you see, smell, taste, hear, and feel on your skin. We should be using our senses to promote the feeling of mindful togetherness with our partner regardless of whether we're performing an ongoing task or activity with them or having a brief encounter. That could mean focusing on the present to enjoy an outdoor breeze surrounding both of you, or the feel of the fabric of the clothing your partner's wearing as you hug them, or the taste of their lips as you kiss each other goodbye for work.

The more we practice mindful togetherness with our partners, the more often we'll find ourselves "forgetting time" and being able to exist with them totally in the present and in full appreciation of all their qualities, no longer distracted by all the busy things of life. You might find yourself having this experience as you dance with them in the kitchen, as you listen to them bare their soul on a particular topic, as you smell their hair while you snuggle in front of a rainy window, or as you make love together.

Connection Strategy 3: Cultivate Honest Conversation

Dr. Jennifer Howard, a relationship expert, says that disconnection happens to couples when one party stops listening to the other, often as a result of their feeling bogged down by life's demands (but you already know this). She goes on to comment, though, that to nourish connection, couples must release their inhibitions and speak clearly and truthfully about their feelings: "When you speak from your heart, it's a bonding opportunity. It's a moment to be real with each other. When we're real with friends, family, partners—anybody—we give them permission to be real, too."[5]

Joe and Samantha were an example of an unwillingness to share feelings with a partner nearly ending in separation.

Joe and Samantha were together but not *in* a relationship; they were overall agreeable to one another but no longer in love. After five years married, it could be said that Joe and Samantha handled co-parenting efficiently, but this functioned in a purely mechanical way. Meanwhile, the couple gave up on acknowledging each other at arrivals or departures, sharing stories about their day or jokes they had heard, or even sharing a bedroom. They stopped engaging in leisure activities together, Samantha enjoying her free time at the gym and trips with friends; and Joe escaping in golf during the summer and in coaching his son's hockey team during the winter.

What Samantha could not have known at the time was that Joe, a financial planner who chronically worried about their future, had been deeply frustrated with Samantha's spending habits for years, feeling as if she was prioritizing enjoying the present over securing a safe and secure retirement. Meanwhile, what Samantha refused to express to Joe was that she felt he had become an overly cautious, uninspired partner who made no effort to bring excitement and surprise into their relationship. As time went on, and as each partner took no initiative to express their feelings to one another, Joe became more and more distraught with a sense that there was a hole inside of him. He began to flirt with an older woman at work and chose to confide in her to express his feelings. What Joe could not know at this time was that Samantha had begun her own fling with a man she met at her gym, who himself confided in Samantha about his own unhappiness in his marriage.

While Joe and Samantha wished that it could've been a different event that led them to start sharing their feelings again, it was a fight in front of one of their children about who would cancel their own activity to stay home for a visit from a plumber that broke open the doors to vulnerability, saving a marriage that was moments away from falling completely apart.

When the couple witnessed the shocked and scared expression on their child's face, they each found themselves pausing. They apologized to their child and ensured them that everything was okay. That day, Joe and Samantha decided to both stay home for the maintenance visit.

After the plumber left, the couple sat down at their kitchen table and agreed how much they disliked having fought in front of their child and upset them. They admitted to each other that they felt disconnected and were scared to be honest with each other—but it had been so long that they still felt inhibited to go much deeper with their feelings, each fearing that they'd be dismissed, criticized, misunderstood, resented, or that they'd just come out feeling foolish.

When I met Joe and Samantha they recounted this story. I explained to them that while they might have been successful parents, friends to their community, and good employees at work, they neglected each other's innate drive to share themselves intimately with one another, resulting in becoming vulnerable to all the *wrong* impulses and attractions.

The subject of being "real" with your significant other is especially difficult for couples who have suffered ongoing, long-term emotional disconnection. There was a time when they were confident in sharing their greatest fears, but now their "honesty muscles" have atrophied so much that they cannot find the strength to authentically connect through mutual openness.

This is why climbing back up the ladder to honest conversation with your partner takes three careful and patient steps, which we'll go over now. As we've learned in previous Days, however, before engaging in any process of repair, we should first agree with our partners on a time in which we both feel comfortable to begin. We can think back on previous guidance to remember that we should not approach each other with "I" statements, but rather with empathetic and compassionate invitations such as "Do you have a few minutes to talk about . . . ?" or "Is this a good time to discuss . . . ?"

Steps to Honest Conversation

7. *Focus on feelings.* At the agreed upon time, partners should take turns explaining their feelings and concerns with the shared understanding that the space carved out for conversation is safe from criticism, secured by trust and understanding, and that the constant goal is to

reestablish connection. We can refer back to previous guidance to formulate our statements in a compassionate, patient, and sincere way: "I worry that we don't allow time to relax and have fun," "When you grab your phone as soon as we sit on the couch, it makes me feel . . . " The temptation is to keep explaining or waffling without hearing from your significant other. Relax and stay focused with the confidence that you have made an important step.

8. *Sincerely listen.* You and your partner may not be having identical experiences of disconnection; as a result, when you bring up the topic, it's possible that they could respond with defensiveness, resulting in accusations or criticism. In any case, your best—and only— response is to listen with curiosity and ask questions in an empathetic manner that reminds the other that your goal is to work together to fix your broken connection. Once you've expressed your feelings and concerns, thanking your partner for listening to you will help ensure that they know how much you appreciate their attention and their respect for your feelings. With the same care and consideration you introduce your issues to your partner, take the same approach to planning a next step or a follow-up discussion with them, with language such as "Do you feel okay talking about this again tomorrow or over the weekend to make sure we're both on the same page?" or "How do you feel about beginning to plan that weekend getaway together?"

9. *Embrace vulnerability.* American professor, social worker, and author Brené Brown, well-known for her explorations on vulnerability, says that in collecting thirteen thousand pieces of data over twelve years, the consistent theme she's discovered is that courage and vulnerability are inextricably linked. In other words, your decision to speak up and express your feelings to others is powered by a willingness to face uncertainty, especially as far as how the other person will respond. Speaking up about your feelings to your significant other may in fact be the most courageous act of your relationship, especially since the alternative is "easy." Being vulnerable is most difficult as it is an expression that we are not perfect. But as the songwriting poet

Leonard Cohen once wrote, "There's a crack, a crack in everything / That's how the light gets in."

Of course, the successful outcome of an honest conversation depends on your partner's willingness to open up honestly themselves—but they may not yet have the courage to be vulnerable, or are not yet able to appreciate the long-term value of being open together. So, what's next in this situation?

This is the time to understand the roots of your partner's fears. Perhaps they've been conditioned to rejection from romantic partners, or to believe that they are unlovable. Did they grow up in a home where it was necessary to build walls, fearing they wouldn't be loved, and learning to push away any overtures of affection? Had they been significantly hurt in a previous relationship?

If you are unsuccessful in helping your partner to understand the walls they've put up around them and break through, it is highly advised to seek professional counseling. In the meantime, you can continue to speak honestly and compassionately with your partner and make it a priority to seek understanding and show empathy.

While outsiders may be able to identify signs of connection and disconnection in others' relationships more easily than those in the relationship themselves—a symptom of being "too close" to the subject at hand—we can all become better and better at identifying the signs of disconnection by reviewing the stark inverse relationship that connection and disconnection share.

Connection is powered by ARMS—being available, responsive, caring, and close to our partners.

Disconnection is powered by unavailability, distance, and an unwillingness to confide in our partners.

Connection shows itself in actions, words, and body language that communicate empathy and security.

Disconnection shows itself in withdrawal, distraction, accusations, and criticism.

Connection lets the other person hear "You care about me."

Disconnection lets the other person hear "You are not important."

Connection is perpetuated by gestures of reassurance and follow-through.

Disconnection is perpetuated by unwillingness to compromise and lack of devotion.

Connection promotes contentment through mutual acceptance of flaws and celebration of assets.

Disconnection promotes discontentment through unrealistic desires and requests.

Connection inspires hope and optimism.

Disconnection inspires anger, hostility, and anxiety.

Connection is built on the sharing of interest.

Conclusion: Love Is Meant to Last

Love is meant to last—it *wants* to and it *needs* to. But too often our intimate relationships cannot survive all the "damage" we've incurred in our past, whether relating to our upbringing or to previous unhealthy relationships, or, as is naturally often the case, both.

The beauty of forging a lasting, loving bond with another person, however, is that it can truly repair so much of that damage we can't seem to shake and help us build the rest of our lives in ways we couldn't have imagined. In a bond of lasting love, we can help each other heal our past wounds, regardless of how they were brought to us, and set ourselves on a path toward emotional well-being that impacts all other aspects of our lives.

We should all be equally motivated to build and sustain a long-term, loving relationship as it gives us the special opportunity to provide stability, well-being, and a sense of real meaning and purpose to the life of another person who is on a similar journey of healing.

We have spent the last twenty-one days exploring what it means to build a loving relationship, and we have learned that it takes real work—all relationships take work, especially those that seem more "perfect" than others.

So let's talk one more time about the work. As you continue to review the strategies and exercises across this guide and apply those that resonate most with you and your partner, you should keep in mind three essential things about the work required to ensure a loving, lasting relationship.

Collaboration Is the Key

At all times, you and your partner should be making decisions and setting goals together, in consensus. In a relationship, consensus that leads to progress often requires compromise and a resetting of expectations. What's more, collaboration is rendered successful only with follow-through.

Partners must be vigilant in helping each other fight off the enemies of follow-through. One of the three main enemies of follow-through is negative self-talk, the kind of internal voice that says things like, "It's too hard. It won't work. It's too late. Why me?" The second most formidable enemy is expecting too much, too soon. But in dedicated collaboration with our partner, we can help each other fight these enemies and remain on the path to lasting love.

Beliefs Can (and Often Should) Be Reconsidered

Biologically, our brains equip us all with the ability to constantly change our perspectives through the gift of neuroplasticity, defined by Encyclopædia Britannica as the "capacity of neurons and neural networks in the brain to change their connections and behavior in response to new information, sensory stimulation, development, damage, or dysfunction."[1] If our old neural networks have reinforced untrue, irrational, and illogical beliefs, then it is vital for us to prompt new, reality-based, rational goal-directed beliefs, which can result in a total pivot of our emotional responses. You can do this in practicing all of the guidance we've reviewed for staging open, honest, empathetic, goal-oriented conversation.

In my own experience counseling couples in healthy and productive conversation, I have witnessed thought transformations from untrue, irrational beliefs to reality-based, rational, goal-directed beliefs, such as these:

- *She doesn't care about what I need or notice how much I do. At least my friends and coworkers appreciate me.*
  - *I never realized my being away caused her to shut down, and I never truly considered just how much she deserves credit for. I am ready to put our relationship first.*
- *He lies about why he doesn't want to spend time with me. He can't be trusted. I don't think I can have a life with him anymore.*
  - *I can see now how scared he was to share his true feelings with me, since I often responded with such anger and criticism. But he just wanted to ask for a little more space on the weekends to engage in his own hobbies. I am absolutely willing to give him this—after all, he lets me spend time with my reading group on Friday evenings, and he always puts the kids first!*

Sometimes, all it takes is a single productive conversation to flip like a pancake an untrue preconception to a reality-based understanding. From there, not only is the path to real problem-solving laid, but partners may begin to feel like they really "know" each other again and can begin to rebuild their intimate connection.

The Difference Is Made in Practice

When we do the work of reconsidering harmful, untrue beliefs and convert them to reality-based ones, we must care for our new beliefs like fragile birds who need time to practice navigating the world. Our old beliefs were fortified through repeating them in our minds, likely over many years, and these thoughts translated into our well-practiced behaviors. We must "practice" our new beliefs every day with our actions, helping them to grow stronger and stronger to the point that our old beliefs disappear entirely, like vapor burning off of our minds.

As we begin to give our new beliefs practice, we should be prepared for our old beliefs to attempt to butt back into the conversation, so to speak. We can fend off these old beliefs, though, by staying calm and thoughtful, and remembering to treat our partner (and ourselves) with compassion. Think of this challenge in terms of what happens after you rehang a door in your house to swing open the opposite way. You have built up a muscle memory for that door, so that when you approach it, you still want to open it in the original direction. It takes repeated encounters with that door to shift your muscle memory so that you reflexively begin to open it the new way. In the meantime, we should forgive ourselves when we find ourselves still reflexively engaging with our old beliefs, which are so used to having power in our minds.

If there's one thing I hope you can take from this guide, it's that when we make the decision to change our perspectives—and thus our behaviors—with our partners, we can truly transform our relationships in ways that felt impossible yesterday, if not minutes ago. That when we work together with our partners to *stop* the relationship train we're on and have the courage to board a new one, the quality of our relationships can suddenly shift from mediocre—if not destructive—to magical and truly transformative. It's magical when we break through all the barriers that have been keeping us from really *seeing* our partners for who they are; it's magical when healthy conversation allows us to open new doors of insight we never thought possible; it's magical to realize how strong giving, rather than taking, makes us; and it's magical to realize the person you set out to build your life with is not only here to stay, but here to support you, guide you, heal you, understand you, and truly love you into the everlasting future.

Acknowledgements

This book began in the late 1990s and combines more than twenty-five thousand hours of face-to-face client meetings with the wisdom of thinkers and researchers in the fields of psychology, philosophy, and spirituality. It is the culmination of a dream, but none of it would be possible without the help of my clients who tested this material and gave me feedback and encouragement.

In its earliest form, this project was a place to share the most successful strategies for building and healing a couple's relationship. It would never have gone further than the many documents on my desktop but for two women who believed this was something the world wanted and needed. My friend Rachelle Bernardi was the original proofreader and editor, and my assistant and soon-to-be friend, Victoria Theodoridis, was the cheerleader who reached out to agents and publishers tirelessly. I couldn't pay either of you enough for being in my life at that moment.

While growing her real estate practice in Southwestern Ontario and navigating her life as a thirty-something, Rachelle took time out to read and format every page of my manuscript, while testing my ideas with her friend group.

Victoria began as an intern and introduced me to social media, taking my next steps before I could.

If my husband is the rock by my side, my children and grandchildren bring the music. They have shaped and supported me, and I am more because of them.

A huge thanks to my publisher, Milli Brown, for seeing my potential and shepherding *Guide to Lasting Love*. Thanks also to my publishing team, Karen Alley, for seeing the big picture, Ben Davidoff, for your laser focus on good writing, and Mary Winzer for the finishing touches. All I can say is you are all so WOW!

To Alana, Marceline, Susan, Joanne, and the friends who were a sounding board for my ideas. Thank you.

Notes

Introduction

1. Korin Miller, "The Best Relationship Advice, According to Experts," Oprah Daily, January 15, 2019, https://www.oprahdaily.com/life/relationships-love/a25907941/expert-relationship-advice/.

Four Relationship Truths

1. Elliot Aronson, *The Social Animal*, 12th ed. (New York: Worth Publishers, 2018).
2. Robert Augustus Masters, *Spiritual Bypassing: When Spirituality Disconnects Us from What Really Matters* (California: North Atlantic Books, 2010), 22.
3. Carol S. Dweck, *Mindset: The New Psychology of Success* (New York: Random House, 2006).
4. Carol S. Dweck.
5. John Tierney and Roy F. Baumeister, *The Power of Bad: How the Negativity Effect Rules Us and How We Can Rule It* (London: Penguin Press, 2019).

Day 1: Creating a Purpose-Driven Relationship

1. Michaéla C. Schippers and Niklas Ziegler, "Life Crafting as a Way to Find Purpose and Meaning in Life," *PubMed Central* 10 (December 2019): 2778, https://www.ncbi.nlm.nih.gov/pmc/articles/PMC6923189/.
2. Saul McLeod, "Erik Erikson's Stages Of Psychosocial Development," SimplyPsychology, January 25, 2024, https://www.simplypsychology.org/erik-erikson.html.
3. Viktor Frankl, *Man's Search for Meaning* (Boston: Beacon Press, 2006).

Day 2 : Finding Hope

1. "Forgiveness: Your Health Depends on It," John Hopkins Medicine, Health entry, site last updated 2024, https://www.hopkinsmedicine.org/health/wellness-and-prevention/forgiveness-your-health-depends-on-it.
2. Nelson Mandela attribution, *Invictus*, directed by Clint Eastwood (Santa Monica, CA: Warner Bros. Pictures, 2009).

Day 3 : Growth Mindset

1. Carol S. Dweck.

Day 4 : Responding to Signals for Attention

1. Logan Ury, "Want to Improve Your Relationship? Start Paying More Attention to Bids," The Gottman Institute, site last updated 2024, https://www.gottman.com/blog/want-to-improve-your-relationship-start-paying-more-attention-to-bids/.
2. C. J. Eubanks Fleming, "Predicting Relationship Help Seeking Prior to a Marriage Checkup," *PubMed Central* 61, no. 1 (February 2012): 90-100, https://www.ncbi.nlm.nih.gov/pmc/articles/PMC3346285/.

Day 5: Making a Match of Different Personalities

1. William J. Chopik and Richard E. Lucas, "Actor, partner, and similarity effects of personality on global and experienced well-being," *Journal of Research in Personality* 78 (2019): 24-261, https://www.sciencedirect.com/science/article/abs/pii/S0092656618301508?via%3Dihub.

2. Amanda Glynn, "The Psychology of Romance: The Impact of Personality Traits on Romantic Relationships," *Inquiries* 11, no. 12 (2019), http://www.inquiriesjournal.com/a?id=1776.

Day 6: Ending Couple Wars

1. Howard E. LeWine, "Understanding the stress response," Harvard Health Publishing, April 3, 2024, https://www.health.harvard.edu/staying-healthy/understanding-the-stress-response.

2. Lian Bloch et al., "Emotion regulation predicts marital satisfaction: More than a wives' tale," *NIH* 14, no. 1 (February 2014): 130-144, https://pubmed.ncbi.nlm.nih.gov/24188061/.

Day 7: Intentional Communication Strategies

1. Stephen Covey, *7 Habits of Highly Effective People: Powerful Lessons in Personal Change*, (New York: Simon & Schuster, 2020), 239.

Day 8: Moving from I to We

1. Richard Weissbourd et al., "Loneliness in America: How the Pandemic Has Deepened an Epidemic of Loneliness and What We Can Do About It," Harvard Graduate School of Education Making Caring Common Project, February 2021, https://mcc.gse.harvard.edu/reports/loneliness-in-america.

2. "The Decline of Marriage and Rise of New Families," Pew Research Center, Overview entry, November 18, 2010, https://www.pewresearch.org/social-trends/2010/11/18/ii-overview/#:~:text=in%201960%2c%2072%25%20of%20american,in%20the%20past%20half%20century.

3. "Barely Half of U.S. Adults Are Married – A Record Low," Pew Research Center, Social Trends entry, December 14, 2011,

https://www.pewresearch.org/social-trends/2011/12/14/barely-half-of-u-s-adults-are-married-a-record-low/#:~:text=The%20 Pew%20Research%20analysis%20also,for%20the%20past%20 half%20century.

4. Francis Weller, *The Wild Edge of Sorrow: Rituals of Renewal and the Sacred Work of Grief* (California: North Atlantic Books, 2015), 115.

5. Gary Chapman, *The Five Love Languages*, Special Edition (New York: Northfield Publishing, 2015).

6. Lisa Capretto, "Father Richard Rohr On Why Certain Relationships Don't Last," *Huffington Post*, February 5, 2015, https://www.huffpost.com/entry/richard-rohr-relationships-love-last_n_6616892.

7. Harville Hendrix, *Getting the Love You Want: A Guide for Couples* (New York: St. Martin's Griffin, 2019).

8. Harville Hendrix.

Day 9: Dealing with Criticism from Your Partner

1. "Gottman Love Lab and Marathon Therapy," The Gottman Institute, site last updated 2024, https://www.gottman.com/couples/marathon-couples-therapy/.

2. Stan Tatkin, *Wired for Love: How Understanding Your Partner's Brain and Attachment Style Can Help You Defuse Conflict and Build a Secure Relationship*, 2nd ed. (California: New Harbinger Publications Inc., 2024).

3. Stan Tatkin.

4. John Gottman, *The Relationship Cure: A 5-Step Guide to Strengthening Your Marriage, Family, and Friendships* (New York: Three Rivers Press, 2001).

5. Kyle Benson, "The Magic Relationship Ratio, According to Science," The Gottman Institute, last updated 2024, https://www.gottman.com/blog/the-magic-relationship-ratio-according-science/.

Day 10: Addressing Your Own Critical Nature

1. Brad J. Bushman et al., "Does Venting Anger Feed or Extinguish the Flame? Catharsis, Rumination, Distraction, Anger, and Aggressive Responding," *Sage Journals* 6, no. 28 (June 2002), https://journals.sagepub.com/doi/10.1177/0146167202289002.

Day 11: The Three Dos and Don'ts of Problem-Solving

1. Ellie Lisitsa, "Predicting Divorce From The First 3 Minutes of Conflict Discussion," The Gottman Institute, site last updated 2024.

Day 12: The Stubborn Problem

1. Marie-Michèle Boisvert et al., "Couples' Reports of Relationship Problems in a Naturalistic Therapy Setting," *AMFC* 19, no. 4 (September 2011), https://doi.org/10.1177/106648071142004.

Day 13: Reducing Stress in Your Relationship

1. Susan Gonsalves, "'Stress in America' survey shows adults have collective trauma," New England Psychologist, January 2, 2024, https://www.nepsy.com/articles/stress-in-america-survey-shows-adults-have-collective-trauma/#:~:text=Twenty%2Dtwo%20percent%20of%20respondents,from%2034%25%20to%2046%25.

2. Ernest Lawrence Rossi, *The 20-Minute Break* (New York: Tarcher, 1991).

3. "Embracing stress is more important than reducing stress, Stanford psychologist says," Stanford Report, in collaboration with Stanford University, May 7, 2015, https://news.stanford.edu/stories/2015/05/embracing-stress-is-more-important-than-reducing-stress,-stanford-psychologist-says.

4. Marguerite Ward, "A brief history of the 8-hour workday, which changed how Americans work," *CNBC*, May 3, 2017, https://www.cnbc.com/2017/05/03/how-the-8-hour-workday-changed-how-americans-work.html; Adiran Chiles, "The 8:8:8

rule could give us the perfect work-life balance. So why aren't more of us following it?" *The Guardian*, site last updated 2024, https://www.theguardian.com/commentisfree/2021/mar/25/the-888-rule-could-give-us-the-perfect-work-life-balance-so-why-arent-more-of-us-following-it.

Day 14: 5 Tips for Staying on Track

1. Bella DePaulo, *Behind the Door of Deceit* (South Carolina: CreateSpace, 2009); Lisa Firestone, "Do You Have an Honest Relationship?" PsychAlive, site last updated 2024, https://www.psychalive.org/do-you-have-an-honest-relationship/#:~:text=While%20people%20seem%20to%20tell,involve%20people's%20closest%20relationship%20partners.

2. William Shakespeare, *Hamlet*, Folger Shakespeare Library, Act 1, Scene 3, 84-6, https://folger.edu/explore/shakespeares-works/hamlet/read/.

3. Mary Beth Sievens, "Divorce, Patriarchal Authority, and Masculinity: A Case from Early National Vermont," *Journal of Social History* 37, no. 3 (2004): 651–61, https://www.jstor.org/stable/3790157.

4. John Thoburn, "Acceptance: The Foundation of Lasting Relationships," Psychology Today, December 10, 2012, https://www.psychologytoday.com/us/blog/he-saidshe-said/201212/acceptance-the-foundation-lasting-relationships.

5. Stephen Covey, *7 Habits of Highly Effective People: Powerful Lessons in Personal Change* (New York: Simon & Schuster, 2020), 71.

Day 15: The Unconscious Agenda

1. Saul Mcleod, "Freud's Theory Of The Unconscious Mind," SimplyPsychology, January 25, 2024, https://www.simplypsychology.org/unconscious-mind.html.

2. Courtney E. Ackerman, "What is Attachment Theory? Bowlby's 4 Stages Explained," PositivePsychology, April 27, 2018, https://positivepsychology.com/attachment-theory/.

3. R. Chris Fraley, "Adult Attachment Theory and Research: A Brief Overview," University of Illinois at Urbana-Champaign Department of Psychology, lab post on personal website, 2018, site last updated 2024, http://labs.psychology.illinois.edu/~rc-fraley/attachment.htm#:~:text=Hazan%20and%20Shaver%20noted%20that,when%20the%20other%20is%20inaccessible.

4. H. F. Harlow et al., "Total social isolation in monkeys," *PNAS* 54, no 1 (July 1965): 90-97,

5. Ji Yoen Lee et al., "Development of the child's ego strength scale: an observation-based assessment of the board game behaviors in play therapy in Korea," *BioMed Central* 15, no. 20 (April 2021), https://capmh.biomedcentral.com/articles/10.1186/s13034-021-00369-3.

Day 16: A Deeper Look at Unmet Needs

1. Phillip Moffit, "The Tyranny of Expectations," Dharma Wisdom, site last updated 2024, https://dharmawisdom.org/the-tyranny-of-expectations/.

2. Jade Wu, "5 Ways to Use Positive Self-Talk to Psych Yourself Up," Psychology Today, March 25, 2021, https://www.psychologytoday.com/us/blog/the-savvy-psychologist/202103/5-ways-to-use-positive-self-talk-to-psych-yourself-up.

3. "What Is Mirror Work?" Louise Hay, https://www.louisehay.com/what-is-mirror-work/.

Day 17: Working through Relationship Stages

1. Richard Rohr, *Essential Teachings on Love*, Modern Spiritual Masters series (New York: Orbis, 2018).

2. Allison Abrams, "Navigating the 4 Stages of a Relationship," Verywell Mind, June 20, 2024, https://www.verywellmind.com/the-four-stages-of-relationships-4163472#:~:text=How%20long%20does%20the%20romantic,10%20or%2015%20years%20later.

3. Katherine Wu, "Love, Actually: The science behind lust, attraction, and companionship," Science in the News, in collaboration with

Harvard Graduate School of Arts and Sciences, February 14, 2017, https://sitn.hms.harvard.edu/flash/2017/love-actually-science-behind-lust-attraction-companionship/.

4. Helen Fisher, *Why We Love: The Nature and Chemistry of Romantic Love* (New York: Holt Paperbacks, 2005), 75.

Day 18: Five Strategies to Sex and Intimacy

1. Sheri Stritof, "How Important Is Sex in a Relationship?" Verywell Mind, March 21, 2023, https://www.verywellmind.com/why-should-you-have-sex-more-often-2300937#:~:text=Why%20 is%20sex%20important%20in,sleep%2C%20and%20boosting%20 immune%20function.

2. Tarra Bates-Duford, "Romantic Relationships Following Childhood Sexual Abuse," PsychCentral, December 25, 2019, https://psychcentral.com/blog/ending-silence/2019/12/romantic-relationships-following-childhood-sexual-abuse#1.

3. Laura Ceci, "Pornography and adult content consumption among men in the United States as of March 2022, by age group," Statista, March 20, 2023, https://www.statista.com/statistics/1375505/ pornographic-consumption-among-us-men-by-age-group/.

4. Misha Duncan Crawford, "Women's Response to Spousal Pornography Use: A Grounded Theory," Master's Thesis (Brigham Young University, 2022), https://scholarsarchive.byu. edu/cgi/viewcontent.cgi?article=10562&context=etd.

5. "Watching pornography rewires the brain to a more juvenile state," The Conversation, November 27, 2019, https://theconversation. com/watching-pornography-rewires-the-brain-to-a-more-juvenile-state-127306.

Day 19: Intimacy Is More Than Sex

1. Anik Debrot et al., "More Than Just Sex: Affection Mediates the Association Between Sexual Activity and Well-Being," *Sage Journals* 43, no. 3 (January 2017), https://doi.org/10.1177/ 014616721668412.

2. Eva-Maria Simms, "Intimacy and the face of the other: A philosophical study of infant institutionalization and deprivation," *Emotion, Space and Society* 13 (November 2014): 80-86, https://www.sciencedirect.com/science/article/abs/pii/S1755458613001060?via%3Dihub.

3. Netherlands Institute for Neuroscience – KNAW, "New study highlights the benefit of touch on mental and physical health," ScienceDaily, April 8, 2024, www.sciencedaily.com/releases/2024/04/240408130610.htm.

4. George Szasz, "The Science of Holding Hands," *BCMJ*, September 26, 2023, https://bcmj.org/blog/science-holding-hands#:~:text=In%20practical%20terms%2C%20hand%2Dholding,to%20express%20feelings%20of%20closeness; Dacher Keltner, "Hands On Research: The Science of Touch," *Greater Good Magazine*, September 29, 2010, https://greatergood.berkeley.edu/article/item/hands_on_research.

5. Yasmin Anwar, "Creating love in the lab: The 36 questions that spark intimacy," UC Berkeley News, February 15, 2015, https://news.berkeley.edu/2015/02/12/love-in-the-lab/; Orion Jones, "36 questions designed to help you fall in love with anyone," *Big Think*, January 12, 2015, https://bigthink.com/surprising-science/how-to-fall-in-love-36-questions-and-deep-eye-contact/.

Day 20: Happiness Is Not Automatic

1. L. J. Hanifan, "The Rural School Community Center," *AAPSS* 67, no 1 (September 1916), https://doi.org/10.1177/000271621606700118.

Day 21: Connection Is the Key

1. Kirsten Gravningen et al., "Reported reasons for breakdown of marriage and cohabitation in Britain: Findings from the third National Survey of Sexual Attitudes and Lifestyles (Natsal-3)," *Plos One* 12, no 3 (March 2017): e0174129, https://journals.plos.org/plosone/article?id=10.1371/journal.pone.0174129.

2. Sue Johnson, "Hold Me Tight," Psychology Today, January 1, 2009, https://www.psychologytoday.com/us/articles/200901/hold-me-tight.

3. Harville Hendrix, *Getting the Love You Want: A Guide for Couples* (New York: St. Martin's Griffin, 2019).

4. Anuradha Baminiwatta and Indrajith Solangaarachchi, "Trends and Developments in Mindfulness Research over 55 Years: A Bibliometric Analysis of Publications Indexed in Web of Science," *PubMed Central* 12, no. 9 (July 2021): 2099-2116, https://www.ncbi.nlm.nih.gov/pmc/articles/PMC8282773/.

5. Wendy R. G., "4 awkward relationship issues that are totally normal," Headspace, site last updated 2024, https://www.headspace.com/articles/awkwardly-normal-relationship-issues.

6. Brené Brown, "The Gifts Of Imperfection," interview by Chad Owen and Mike Parsons, *Moonshots* podcast, episode 62, site last updated 2022, https://www.moonshots.io/episode-62-brene-brown-gifts-of-imperfection-transcript.

Conclusion: Love Is Meant to Last

1. Michael Rugnetta, "Neuroplasticity (biology)," Britannica, last updated June 07, 2024, https://www.britannica.com/science/neuroplasticity.

About the Author

Reta Faye Walker is a seasoned relationship expert with a passion to guide couples into a conscious relationship. Her curiosity about the delicate nuances of human connections was sparked in her earliest years and grew as she navigated the pain of her divorce.

Since then, Reta has spent hundreds of hours pursuing an understanding of human behavior as a student of social sciences, psychology, philosophy, spirituality, marriage, and family. Before *Lasting Love*, she utilized her knowledge to self-publish a book for families going through transitions in modern times.

In addition to writing weekly articles on relationships, in her free time Reta enjoys jogging, lifting weights, practicing yoga, meditating daily, eating good food, and watching as many musicals as possible. Reta has a special love for noisy family gatherings and hanging out with her husband.